COLOUR AND TEXTURE IN THE BRASS BAND SCORE

RAY STEADMAN-ALLEN

Salvationist Publishing and Supplies, Ltd
1 Tiverton Street, London SE1 6NT

© The Salvation Army 1980
First Published 1980
Reprinted 2005
ISBN 0 85412 365 2

PREFACE

Lieut-Colonel (Dr) Ray Steadman-Allen was born on the 18th Sept 1922 to Salvation Army officer parents. When they were appointed to London in 1937 he obtained a job at International Head Quarters as office boy to General Evangeline Booth, daughter of The Salvation Army's founder.

In 1942 he enlisted in the Royal Navy. He was examined for a music diploma by Sir Granville Bantock who invited him to apply for a job in music after the war. In the event, Bantock died, and Ray joined the Music Editorial Department of the Salvation Army. Following a short postwar period as a trombonist with the International Staff Band, he developed his conducting skills, and was Bandmaster of the Tottenham Citadel (later Enfield) Band. His first piece of published music was a march called *Gladsome Morn*, written in 1945.

Much of his music was ahead of its time, to the point that it was sometimes considered unacceptable to the listener. *Lord of the Sea* created furore! His creative genius has been given totally to God, and has been instrumental in guiding Salvation Army music into uncharted territory, particularly when the International Music Editorial Department was under his leadership between 1967 and 1980.

Besides over 200 published brass band pieces for The Salvation Army, he has written numerous choral works with a large number of compositions and arrangements in manuscript, often completed for recordings or special concert presentations. A number of works have been used as test pieces including *Seascapes, Stantonbury Festival, Amaranth, The Beacons* and *Hymn at Sunrise*, as well as a sizeable body of works for wind band including *A Cambridge Triptych*.

Besides completing his doctorate in music, he holds several honorary fellowships, is the President of the National College of Music, Vice President of the Brass Band Conductor's Association, and patron of the London Musicological Research Society.

His contribution to the music world, and especially The Salvation Army continues to be exceptional. He was honoured in June 2005 to be admitted to the Order of the Founder, the highest possible recognition for a Salvationist.

CONTENTS

FOREWORD

INTRODUCTION

PART 1 COLOUR

Chapter 1 COLOUR RESOURCE (1): PURE TONES
Colour resource in general. Pure (like) tones classified by group. Tension and relaxation. Ensembles—'trumpet' family. Ensembles—'saxhorn' family. Pure tones in contrast.

Chapter 2 COLOUR RESOURCE (2): MIXED TONES
Doubling. Combining quartet groups.

Chapter 3 THE FULL BAND
Chord voicing. The *tutti*.

Chapter 4 STANDARD FULL-BAND LAY-OUT OF A HYMN TUNE
Transposition. Allocation of basic parts. Allocation of remaining parts. A hymn tune scored.

Chapter 5 THE TUTTI
'Choral' scoring. 'Group' scoring. The small band.

Chapter 6 GENERAL ENSEMBLES

Chapter 7 SOLO PASSAGES
Solo passages and backgrounds.

Chapter 8 MELODIC LINES
Melodic strands. Inner melodic lines. Reinforced phrase or figure. Range and overlapping. A sustained pedal. Sustained binding tones.

Chapter 9 SPECIAL EFFECTS
Simulated *pizzicato*. Pointed chords. *Forte-piano*. *Glissando*. 'Rip'. Lip trill. Lip *Arpeggio*. Tremolo. Enharmonic tremolo. Flutter tonguing. The 'pyramid'. *Ad lib* (random notes). Mutes.

Chapter 10 PERCUSSION
Snare drum. Bass drum. Timpani. Cymbals. Triangle. Tambourine. Xylophone. Glockenspiel and vibraphone. Celeste. Bells or chimes. Block.

PART 2 TEXTURE

Chapter 11 TEXTURE
Degree of density. Reliefs. Contrapuntal textures. Canon. Counter-melody. *Ostinato*.

Chapter 12 SIX EXAMPLES OF THEMATIC TREATMENT

Chapter 13 FUGAL TEXTURES

Chapter 14 VARIOUS TEXTURES
Jazz or rock scoring. Tune with strong rhythmic backing. Complex structures. Colour variants within a single chord.

Chapter 15 IDIOM
Diatonic writing. Chromaticism and dissonance. Dissonance produced by superimposition.

EPILOGUE

ACKNOWLEDGEMENTS

FOREWORD

I AM glad to recommend this admirable and greatly needed a book, first of all to students, who will find in it not only instructions but also much to stimulate the imagination; and then to musicians working in other realms of the art, as well as discerning listeners. There will be those among them who perhaps do not yet realise the value of the brass band as a vehicle for fine music-making.

The band as it is considered here was a uniquely British institution, evolved in this country over the last 100 years or more, but known and appreciated world wide.

The author's own great talent and experience as a composer is unquestioned, and his teaching in these pages is not only basically sound but also imaginative. For him the band is not merely 'sounding brass', but a sensitive instrument for colour and expression.

ERIC BALL

What, then is colour in music? The term has really a twofold meaning. There is firstly, colour in the sense of variety of expression, and of the timbre of quality of sound which underlies the variety in a single instrument...

The other kind of colour we shall term 'collective'. It is produced by the combination of the timbre of different instruments and their contrast to each other.

Individual colour is the sole property of the executive artist; the composer has no control over it on paper. He can spoil the effect of the composer's colouring by inferior playing, but he cannot alter its inherent qualities. The picture may be hung in a bad light but its value remains the same.

Charles Villiers Stanford, *Musical Composition*.
(McMillan & C and Stainer & Bell)

COLOUR AND TEXTURE IN THE BRASS BAND SCORE

INTRODUCTION

COLOUR

THE brass band, it is sometimes said, lacks colour variety due to the similarity of the instruments, all except the percussion being brass. Whilst the all-brass combination does not enjoy the obvious and wide distinctions between the instruments of the orchestra or military/concert band, it is by no means devoid of the capacity to achieve a range of colours and shades. As a sound-producing medium, a reasonably competent brass band is flexible and expressive. The most serious limitation is not colour but pitch range, especially upward, having a compass of something less than five octaves. Effects made possible by instrumental characteristics, dynamic variants (volume, modes of attack), mutings and register-intensities all yield variety-potential even in the case of a single brass instrument.

The literature for piano demonstrates that the 'monochrome' of that instrument is no disadvantage: *arpeggii*, chord clusters and pedalled sonorities are among the features which can be employed in the creative process. A series of stylistic qualities are available for exploitation from the crisply percussive to a velvet lyricism.

Fundamentally one family, orchestral strings produce homogeneous blends, contrapuntal complexes, introduce harmonics, stoppings, *pizzicati* and an assortment of effects such as playing above the bridge and with the wood of the bow. Players are called upon to supplement by devices like tapping rhythms.

All these modes of operation afford resources which yield colour. Colour is therefore not merely limited to basic timbres but embraces variously-produced sounds in colour mixed together with modifications or additions made possible by the special features of which the involved instruments are capable. The availability of such characteristics will almost inevitably influence and stimulate the composer's musical thinking.

TEXTURE

ADJECTIVES like 'close-woven', 'rough' or 'silky' are used to decribe texture in fabrics, referring to the way the material is made or its tactile qualities. In musical terms *texture* relates to the way in which notes, lines or patterns are combined (eg, chordal blocks or a melodic thread against a contrasted background). The contrapuntal weaving of parts may be 'open' or tightly-knit and complex. Words like 'thick' or 'transparent' are sometimes encountered in the attempt to describe musical texture.

A lot of simultaneous score activity, of an independent nature, can create an impression of busyness—justified in a concentration of combined parts of character (eg, a fugue *stretto*) or for programme reasons like Charles Ives' converging bands. A score can be overloaded with decorative bits and pieces, much of which may be lost in the general effect. On the other hand an involved piece of construction may have been carefully judged, the effectiveness of the whole depending upon the delicate weighing of the parts. One should draw a distinction between purposeful combination and unnecessary clutter.

The elements of colour and texture are rarely independent of each other, timbre, tension (*tessitura*) and notation (values, staccato, etc) being linked with part lay-out. For instance, an important 'line' in a contrapuntal passage might be scored with a particular colour in mind, eg, unison horns. The context of other instruments playing at the same time will have an effect on the relative prominence of the horns—a matter of balance. The element of tension is contributory in that the horn group has stronger speaking power in the upper register (leaving out a further complication, at this stage, of dynamic markings).

Texture has a degree of control over the way in which instrumental colour retains its identity or is lost in the general mass. Take the illustration of a flugel supported by three trombones. In theory there are two sound streams: the flugel sound and the trombone sound. The texture is the manner of employment:

Example 1 (a) The flugel is joined by the trombones in choral style: here the flugel is likely to be heard only as a component of a quartet, its sound blending with the trombones.
        (b) The flugel becomes more identifiable if there is some distance (in register) from the trombones; also the sustained chords unify the trombones and give a feeling of independence to them.
        (c) The flugel's cohesive line stands well out from the trombones' detached chords and rhythmic patterns. In this example both streams are easily differentiated. The basic colours have not altered; the texture has.

Example 1
Silesian folk song

(a) Flugel / Trbs.
(b)
(c)

The purpose of the present book is to codify and analyse combinations of instruments, the examples, almost without exception, being taken from published scores. It is sound practice to examine techniques which have been developed out of experience and are therefore practical and effective. There are those who, in recent years, have expressed the thought that standard scoring practice has something to learn from the works of those who—perhaps unfamiliar—come to the band without traditional grounding but with a fresh approach and individual ways of handling the resources. There is much to be said for this view. However, whilst new thinking is stimulating and refreshing, a caution should be uttered against being carried to the extreme of negating tradition altogether under the spell of new messiahs. New messages may well require new language, but one must seek, at least, to examine how much of a new language has roots in the older tradition and how much is the result of imported thinking from other traditions with the danger of weaknesses arising from a superficial or erroneous idea of the old. Occasionally contemporary brass band scores call for players to perform tasks verging on the virtuoso all round the band (eg, 2nd horns and 2nd baritones being given notes at the bottom of their registers that once were preached as 'muddy' or 'thick'). So much in the way of esoteric utterance is going on that one can be lost in a morass of expressions that the older schools may feel to be more than a little suspect. So may many musicians have felt around 1600 when the voice of the 'New Music' was beginning to be heard. Let us keep open minds and have the humility to learn. Time has the ability to separate the wheat from the chaff and if a man can touch our minds and spirits with his utterances his *modus operandi* is not likely to be too much in question.

The previous paragraph suggests that most of the illustrations will be from traditional sources. At the time of producing this book there is a state of experimentation *at a certain level,* the rarified atmospheres of which will be breathed, but the vast body of standard works—which still form the larger part of listening—deserves serious attention because the works are the distillation of the tested practice of some fine minds and also because the *received* brass band sounds are a glorious product of a legitimate music-making medium which is not yet outworn.

It is said—with some truth—that a good band can make anything sound good. Granted that 'good' is relative and a value-judgement there is a danger in relying on scoring technique to disguise or salvage compositional weakness. Some 'music' turns out to be little more than a procession of devices and tricks currently in fashion.

ARRANGING

FINALLY, a few thoughts on arranging. This is not strictly relevant to the subject of the book but as the readership is likely to include many who are interested in this aspect, perhaps the author may be forgiven for mentioning it. When he makes a straight transcription the arranger's task is rather different from the composer's. A composer may well be thinking in terms of his medium throughout the creative processes. Or he could 'arrange' his work when he has produced it in a short score or piano form. Some works these days are actually scored for the composer by someone else. Insofar as an arranger is called upon to 'clothe' a theme, the approach to and development of that arrangement has a lot in common with the imaginative processes of the composer. Much depends upon the context of the finished product. An updated or stylized version of a tune will impose ideas and treatments from 'without', either compatible with the theme or giving it an entirely new identity (eg, a slick, rhythmic version of some old romantic tune). At the other end of the scale is the approach of soaking oneself in the mood and character of the theme and letting it suggest, from 'within', its manner of handling.

Whichever way he chooses to work, the arranger should have a knowledge of styles appropriate to the theme he handles and the capacity to avoid unintentional anachronisms. Brass band arrangements (or transcriptions) of 'classics' are in disfavour with some purists, even in the face of the practice of earlier centuries and noted transcribers like J. S. Bach. (This is not the place to argue the case either way except to note with wry amusement that it often seems to be the *brass band* medium that is unforgivable rather than the practice of arranging in general, which would have to write off Ravel's masterly orchestration of 'Pictures from an exhibition' conceived by Moussorgsky as a piano work.)

Leaving aside such questions, the arranger, ideally, ought to have sufficient musicology to view the band version through the eyes of the composer or his period. It is not too precious to have a standard of aiming to score the work as he believes the composer concerned (or practice of the period) might have handled it had he written it for the band. This supposes an understanding of style and period (and even of a composer's personal characteristics) as well as skill in instrumentation. This cannot be carried too far in the sense that the work might have been written differently for a band and so on, but the principle is worth stating. Solutions have to be found which will convince, and a facet of arranging skill lies in deciding the new terms. Another facet is judging whether the proposed new transcript is justifiable and practical without doing a disservice to the composer. For this reason music depending upon solid outline is usually more apt for transcription than orchestral music which needs colour for its effect or where orchestral colour is a highly important and distinguishing characteristic. It sometimes happens that a band transcription enhances an original. Today's brass band new productions tend toward original compositions rather than transcription, but an arrangement is occasionally required and—at least in private study—time spent in mastering the problems of transfer from one medium to another is bound to contribute towards fluent mastery of instrumentation for the purpose of conveying the ideas of personal composition, should this gift be present.

RAY STEADMAN-ALLEN

THE preparation of this book seems like an anthology of friendship for it is and has been a privilege to enjoy a cordial personal relationship with many of the composers quoted in the examples. I am indebted to Eric Ball for his foreword and for his helpful observations when reading the manuscript. Also to Brindley Boon for the editing and to Mrs Dorothy Gulston for typing my notes. Not least of my blessings is the creatively-enriching and understanding support of Joy, my wife.

R. S.-A.

PART I

COLOUR

Chapter 1 COLOUR RESOURCE—PURE TONES

1 COLOUR RESOURCE IN GENERAL

THE resources at one's disposal are provided and governed by:
  (a) *instrumental tone colour* permitting variations of *sound*;
  (b) forms of production, eg, *martellato, forte-piano* and *glissando* which produce *effects*;
  (c) style and flexibility (agility) permitting variation in *texture*.

Element (a) occurs in a single-instrument sound, the combination of like tones, mixtures of sounds (yielding synthetics), tones standing out in relief from backing tones.

Element (b) will be present in some degree in (c) and is affected by (a). That is to say the patterns and phrases must have tone colour of some kind and will be produced in certain ways, eg, a lyrical passage played *cantabile* by a cornet.

Element (c) will be seen in figurations, patterns and melodic phrases.

These three elements are interactive. They will be discussed in detail in the course of the study. In this chapter element (a)—tone colour—will be considered in terms of *pure tones*: the pure, characteristic sounds of single instruments or when grouped with instruments of like colour. Such groups will also be considered when contrasted with groups of unlike colour.

2 PURE (LIKE) TONES—CLASSIFIED BY GROUP

Though valved brass band instruments (excluding percussion) are technically saxhorns, they can be conveniently grouped into two families:
  (a) the *trumpet* family; cornets E♭ and B♭ (trombones);
  (b) the *horn* family: flugel horn B♭, tenor horn E♭ (alto horn in USA), baritone B♭ (the real *tenor register* instrument), euphonium B♭ and basses (tubas) E♭ and B♭. In brass band nomenclature the flugel horn is usually shortened to 'flugel', the tenor horn to 'horn'. Sometimes bass EE♭ or BB♭ is seen; this refers to the *bore* which is much wider than instruments described as 'single' E♭ and B♭. The result is a deeper sonority, but note that pitch is not affected, the *length* of tube being the same. Inconsistently, the soprano is not shown E♭. The term 'double-B' is often used by bandsmen when speaking of the B♭ bass. Older phraseology refers to the 'bombardon' (E♭ bass) and 'monstre bass' (B♭ bass).

Of the B♭ instruments the cornet and flugel are highest; sounding an octave lower whilst reading the same written pitch are baritone, tenor trombone and euphonium. The B♭ bass sounds two octaves lower than the cornet.

Of the E♭ instruments the soprano cornet (usually called soprano) is highest, being pitched a fourth above the B♭ cornet. The horn is an octave lower than the soprano, the E♭ bass two octaves lower. The relationship between the B♭ and E♭ instruments can be seen in the following scale. (Readers will doubtless be aware that brass band instruments use a non-transposing treble clef—with the exception of the bass trombone whose part is written bass clef concert pitch. Some scores use the tenor clef for tenor trombones.)

Example 2

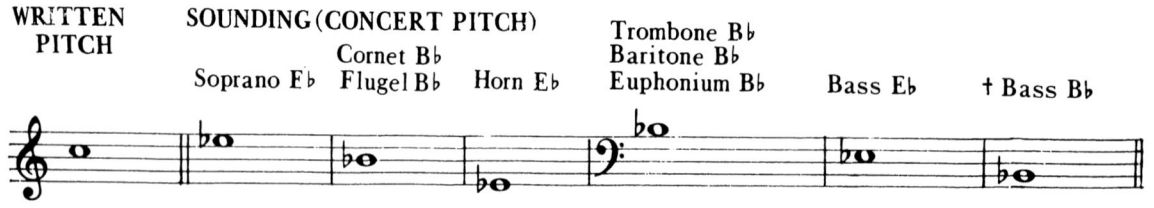

WRITTEN PITCH | SOUNDING (CONCERT PITCH)

Soprano E♭ | Cornet B♭ / Flugel B♭ | Horn E♭ | Trombone B♭ / Baritone B♭ / Euphonium B♭ | Bass E♭ | † Bass B♭

Bass Trombone is scored in bass clef (concert). Trigger G & D now often used or the part played on B♭ & F.
† Sometimes shown as BB♭ and colloquially referred to as 'double - B'.

Whilst there are differences of pitch and timbre between the members of each of the two 'families', the general classification will serve us for practical purposes.

'Trumpet' and 'horn' suggest brightness and mellowness respectively, (the term 'mellows' has been used in the USA to refer to the latter group), but the manner of performance can modify the basic characteristics so that blending is possible to the extent of making the tone colours practically indistinguishable from one another in combination. As with other instrumental aggregates, there does not have to be a sacrificing of individual tone colour in order to blend. The characteristic sound of a *tutti* is produced by the combination of individual characteristic sounds. The point being made here is the capacity of brass to exploit a fair degree of variation of tone colour. Probably brass bands have required far more subtlety of variant in tone colour than has orchestral brass which—on the whole—is (or has been) expected to have a certain invariability of character.

3 TENSION AND RELAXATION

People speak of 'high' or 'low' notes referring to a relative effect on the ear; as vibrations increase in rapidity the note appears to 'rise'. The wail of a siren is probably the most familiar example. Without going deeply into playing techniques, a characteristic phenomenon of brass is that the impression of intensity varies according to the requisite degree of tension or relaxation of the player's lips. The higher the note the greater the intensity and the lower the note, the more relaxed the lip, the less the impression of intensity. As has been said, to some extent this phenomenon is true of the majority of instruments; it is, however, particularly striking in brass.

As an illustration consider [musical notation] (concert pitch).

It will be obvious that the highest pitched instrument, the soprano, will have to play the lowest written note to produce the concert B♭. As the instrument producing this note gets larger and deeper in pitch, so its written note will be correspondingly higher, resulting in increasing intensity.

(All illustrations are the written notes unless otherwise stated.)

Example 3

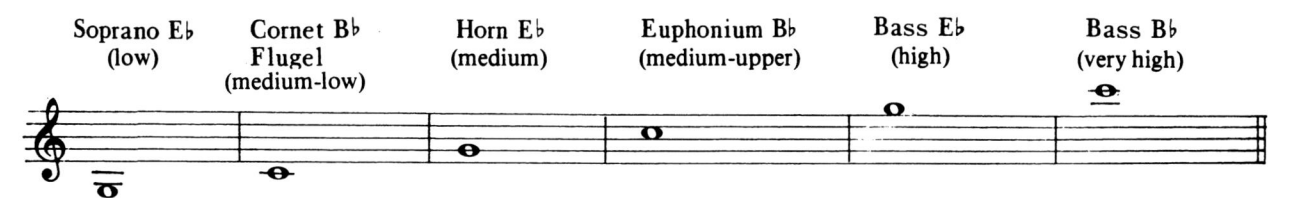

| Soprano E♭ (low) | Cornet B♭ Flugel (medium-low) | Horn E♭ (medium) | Euphonium B♭ (medium-upper) | Bass E♭ (high) | Bass B♭ (very high) |

The soprano is the most relaxed, the B♭ bass the most intense. This characteristic (which has a vocal parallel) adds a range of *intensity colour* to the band, making possible effects which are not always apparent from a mere glance at the score.

Notes at the extremities of register are beginning to be exploited much more than once was the case. Earlier this was doubtless due to the more limited technique of the average player, and even now the commercial practicalities dictate that these and kindred technical difficulties mitigate against effective performance and are reserved for contest pieces or works designed for superbands. Nevertheless notes at the extreme ends of registers are effective when wisely incorporated. 'Pedal C' (B♭ concert) is quite commonplace for trombones. 'Pedal F' has been occasionally encountered for B♭ bass. The rich quality of E♭ bass pedals has infrequently been an ingredient of brass band scoring but they can be a valuable asset.

This book does not intend to cover very much elementary ground already available in books concerned with brass band scoring, notably the late Dr Denis Wright's masterly *Scoring for Brass Band,* but it is pertinent to mention at this point that the medium-to-low register of the E♭ bass is usually preferable, in solo or thin scoring, to the medium register of the B♭ bass which is inclined to sound a little wooden above E on the lowest stave line (brass band written pitch) in all but expert hands. There are, however, effective uses of the B♭ bass in this range:

Example 4 *On the Cornish Coast* (Henry Geehl)

[musical notation: Bass B♭, pp misterioso]

The tenor trombone is a favourite exponent of high register lyricism, one of the influences of 'big band jazz' on the brass band. Coupled with a tremolo obtained by rapid and minute slide movements, the result is a sweet crooning sound. It is a sound wherein the sturdy nobility of the trombone is thoroughly emasculated, but is highly effective, especially in popular idioms.

A group of trombones high in close harmony is a further feature of the same technique:

Example 5

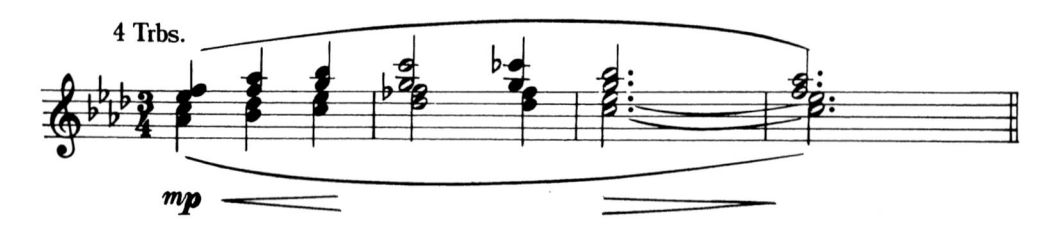

A trio of highly placed trombones produces blazing brilliance:

Example 6 *Energy* (Robert Simpson)

In its upper register the euphonium is capable of intense warmth and vibrancy:

Example 7 *A Carol Fantasy* (Eric Ball)
(G.S. 1562)

The baritone is akin to the horn, but fuller and, of course, deeper with a touch of the more tender and mellow side of the trombone. In the following solo passages the baritone is reminiscent of the orchestral horn:

Example 8 *The Holy War* (R. S.-A.)
(F.S. 298)

At the other end of the scale low-pitched unisons are strong and rich. There are many instances of unison writing; the scores consulted contain unisons from medium low upward. (The full sound of the whole cornet section is striking.)

Example 9 *Prometheus Unbound* (Granville Bantock)

Generally rather rare, however, is the unison in the lowest register. A melody in octaves has a fine sonority, in this instance having the powerful sweep of a string orchestra:

Example 10 *A Moorside Suite* (Gustav Holst)

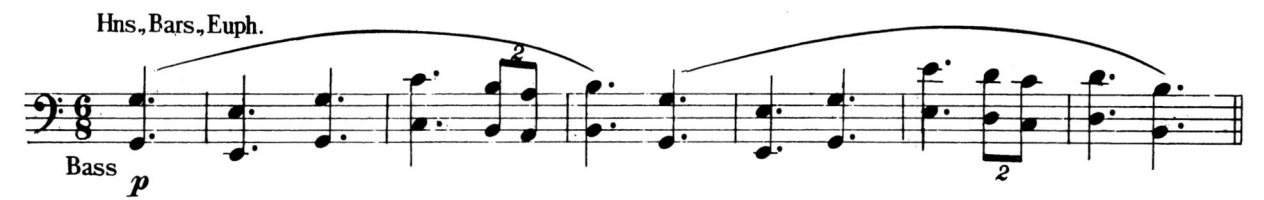

See also Examples 27-30, 54 and 62

Some other unison combinations are baritones + euphonium; trombones; tenor trombones + baritones (+ euphonium); basses (+ euphonium)—unison and in octaves; tenor trombones + euphonium.

The whole cornet line is sometimes split into octaves. The two main ways of dividing are:
(a) soprano + solo cornet—upper line, other cornets lower line;
(b) similar to above but dividing solo cornets as well. Often the flugel horn is co-opted to strengthen the lower line. It blends very well.

4   ENSEMBLES—'TRUMPET' FAMILY

As a rule voicings are in score order. A few typical examples are given.

(a) *Cornets* (standard band: soprano, four solo cornets, one repiano (1st), two 2nd, two 3rd).

(NB: Salvation Army bands do not employ 3rd cornet, flugel always has a separate part, and the term '1st cornet' is used instead of 'repiano'. 'Repiano' has largely become a traditional brass band word—from the Italian *ripieno*. Standard brass band scores other than SA frequently link flugel and repiano cornet, indicating one or other when necessary. The flugel has been treated independently much more in recent years. It is quite common practice to incorporate the flugel into the cornet ensemble where it blends happily and provides, when required, a useful voice in the securing of balance. A few groupings given below therefore include flugel, although technically it is an 'outsider'.)

Having 3rd cornet available.

Three harmony parts

I	S. Ct.	S. Ct.	Rep. + Fl.	Sop. + S. Ct.	Sop. + S. Ct.
II	Rep. + Fl.	S. Ct.	2nd Ct.	S. Ct. + Rep.	Rep. + 2nd Ct.
III	2nd + 3rd Ct.	Rep. + 2nd Ct.	3rd Ct.	S. Ct. + 2nd Ct. (& 3rd)	S. Ct. + 3rd Ct.

Without 3rd cornet (the first, second and fourth examples above are also workable).

Three parts
I   S. Ct. (+ Sop.)
II 1st Ct. + Fl.
III S. Ct. + 2nd Ct.

Other permutations will suggest themselves. The above are all taken from standard works. In three-part harmony there has been a growing tendency to allocate all three notes to the solo cornets as something of an insurance, other parts doubling as required. It is, of course, not always a question of employing the whole section—a trio of cornets may be all that is wanted.

Four parts

Example 11 *I saw three ships* (Brian Bowen)
(F.S. 361)

Five parts

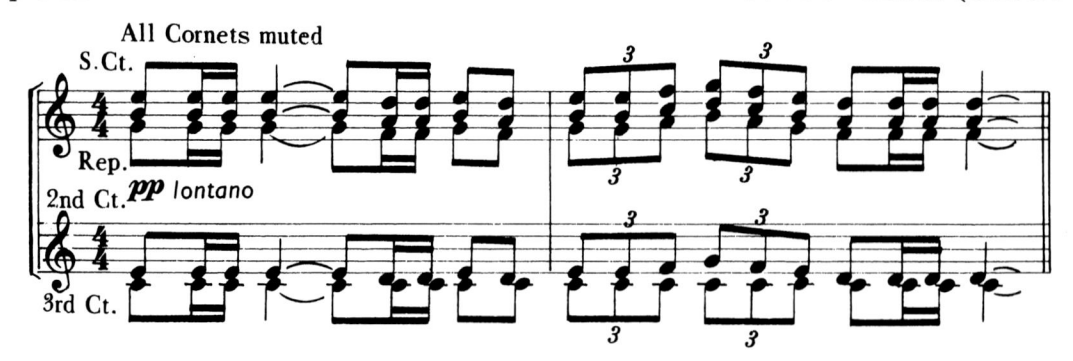

Example 12

John o' Gaunt (Gilbert Vinter)

Assuming that cornet sound alone is required, it is possible that, for five or more parts, one player per part will be adequate, depending upon the context and nature of the music. Where a solid body of corporate sound is called for, the trombones are frequently co-opted:

Example 13

New Frontier (William Himes)
(F.S. 365)

N.B. S.A. score without 3rd cornet. If scored to include 3rd cornet it would usefully reinforce 2nd trombone.

(b) *Trombones* (usually three—two tenors and a bass).

The B♭/F and G/D trombones have greatly facilitated the use of trombones in the band both from the standpoint of what was once awkward slide shifting (first to seventh position, etc) and the obtaining of low-register notes. Three trombones is the invariable rule in non-SA scores; SA scores occasionally print four as there are still quite a number of SA bands which carry a numerical strength of more than the standard 25. At an earlier period a large number of SA bands numbered up to 50 and 60 players. Scores around 1920 carry divided 1st cornets and 1st baritones. The trombone quartet has been a useful feature and the tradition has remained. The extra part is normally cued—usually for 1st baritone which blends well. Possibly conditioned, the author feels that there is a good deal to be said for four trombones; at the same time obviously there is a problem with four-part writing. The value of the baritone, to supply a fourth part, has been mentioned; in 'Resurgam' Eric Ball uses 3rd cornet to make the fourth part in a *pianissimo* trombone passage. The cornet is sandwiched between 1st and 2nd trombone (Example 16).

It is sometimes possible, by exercising a little thought, to ensure a satisfactory three-part harmony, making the fourth part an 'optional' extra. The additional part could be less than ideal academically, but it is worth practical consideration.

Three trombones

Example 14

Toccata (Wilfred Heaton)
(F.S. 354)

Four trombones

Example 15

'Ein' feste burg' from *The Holy War* (R. S.-A.)
(F.S. 298)

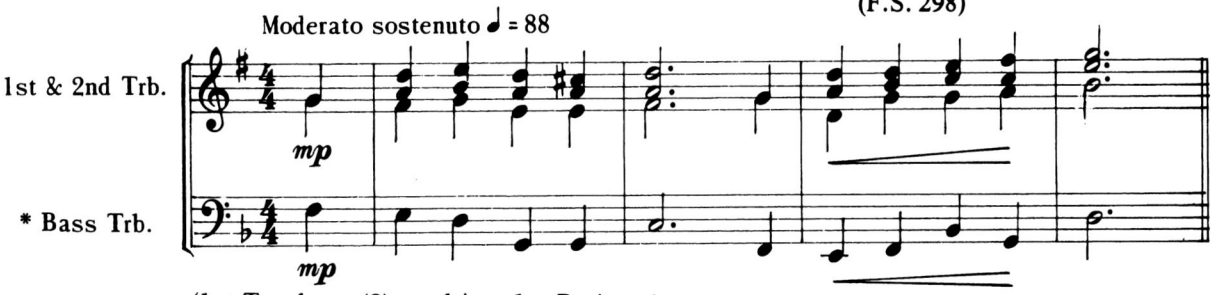

Moderato sostenuto ♩ = 88

1st & 2nd Trb.

* Bass Trb.

(1st Trombone (2) cued into 1st Baritone)

* In the score doubled, largely at the 8ve, by E♭ Bass.

Fourth part supplied by a cornet.

Example 16

Resurgam (Eric Ball)
(F.S. 302)

Allegro ♩. = 80

3rd Ct.

1st & 2nd Trb.

Bass Trb.

(c) *Two cornets, two trombones*

Example 17

Victory (R. S.-A.)
(F.S. 237)

Vivace e leggiero ♩ = 104

Solo Ct.

1st & 2nd Trb.

Bass trombone replaces 2nd trombone if desired.

(d) *Full ensemble of cornets and trombones*

A basic four-part lay-out

Example 18

Melodies of Grieg (arr R. S.-A.)
(F.S. 334)

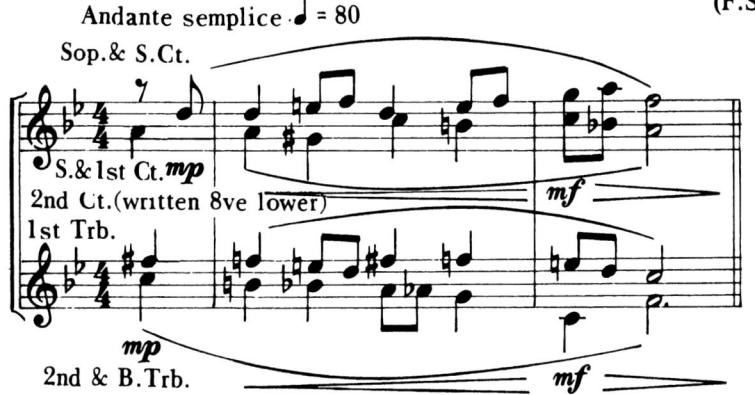

Andante semplice ♩ = 80

Sop. & S.Ct.

S. & 1st Ct.
2nd Ct. (written 8ve lower)
1st Trb.

2nd & B.Trb.

Three-octave scoring of basic two parts over bass trombone pedal:

Example 19 *Variations for brass band* (R. Vaughan Williams)

In the above examples the parts are equally distributed. If a particular line is to be emphasized, more weight (added instrument(s), stronger dynamic) is given to it.

5 ENSEMBLES—'SAXHORN' FAMILY

So many types of instrument compose this group that a great number of combinations are possible. A few of the more usual ones are given with their approximate vocal parallels (soprano, alto, tenor and bass).

(a)	*three parts*	flugel	horn	baritone	S.A.T.
		flugel	horn	horn	S.S.A. or S.A.A.
		horn	baritone	euphonium (E♭ bass)	A.T.B.
(b)	*four parts*	flugel	horn	baritone	euphonium	S.A.T.B.
		flugel	horn	horn	euphonium	S.A.T.B.
		3 horns, baritone.				(close harmony A.T. range)
(c)	*five parts*	flugel, 2 horns, baritone, euphonium S.A.A.T.B. or S.S.A.T.B.
		flugel, horn, 2 baritones, euphonium S.A.T.T.B.
		flugel, horn, baritone, euphonium, bass, S.A.T.B.B.
		2 horns, baritone, euphonium, bass, A.A.T.T.B.

Each of five parts may be real (no strict doubling) or melody or bass may be duplicated at the octave.

The above voicings allocate parts to instruments in approximation to relative register. Illustrated below is the use of the euphonium as the upper part (melody).

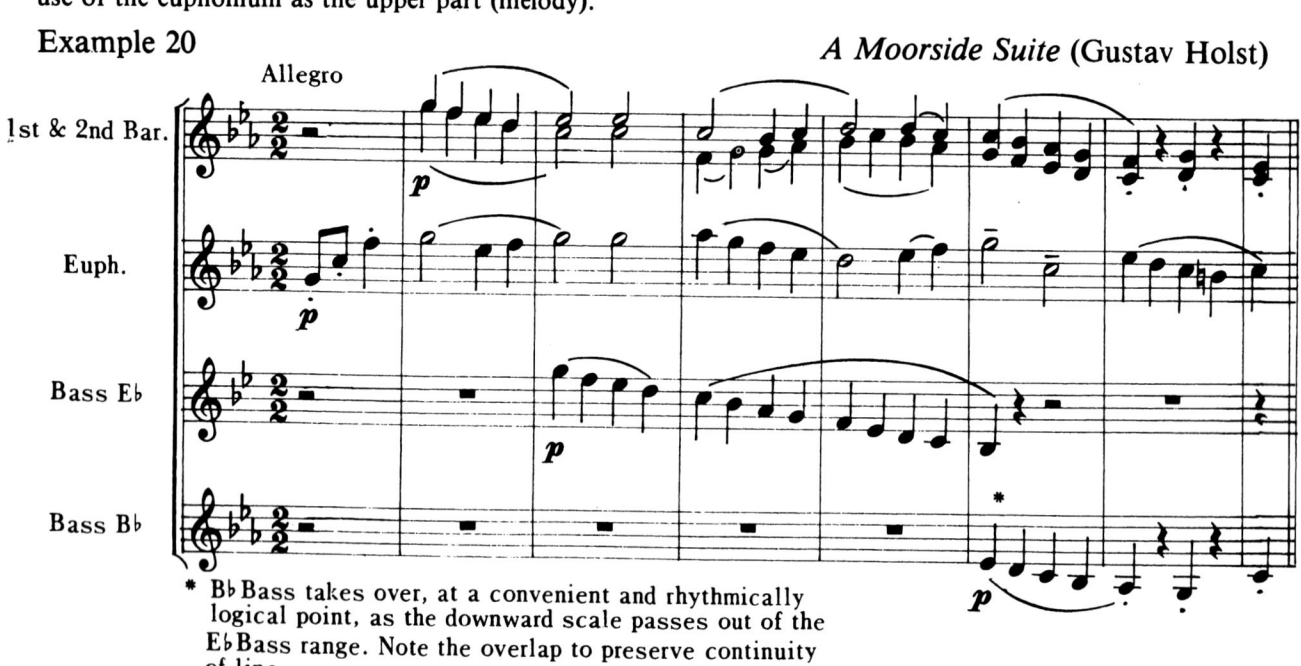

Example 20 *A Moorside Suite* (Gustav Holst)

* B♭ Bass takes over, at a convenient and rhythmically logical point, as the downward scale passes out of the E♭ Bass range. Note the overlap to preserve continuity of line.

'Male voice' groupings are occasionally encountered.

(d) Three trombones and bass.

Two baritones, one euphonium and bass.

Example 21   *A Kensington Concerto* (Eric Ball)

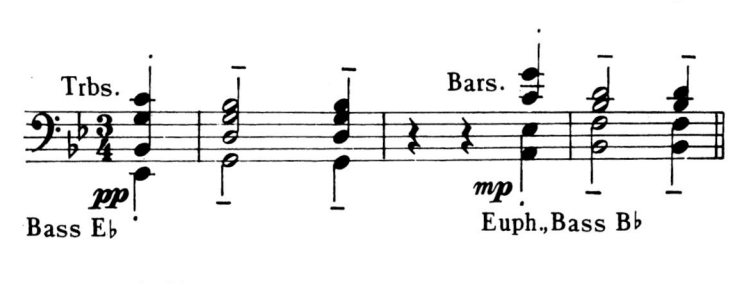

(concert pitch)

Horn, two baritones doubling divided euphoniums, basses (standard band has two pairs of basses):

Example 22   *Notturno Religioso* (Erik Leidzén)
                                                                                (F.S. 355)

(e) 'Tuba quartet'. Of these there are two usual combinations:
        (i) two euphoniums, two basses;
        (ii) four basses.

Example 23   *Music for Tubas* (Michael Kenyon)

A final example shows the complete family of saxhorns employed.

Example 24   *Variations for brass band* (R. Vaughan Williams)

6 PURE TONES IN CONTRAST

The blend and contrast of instrumental sounds are as essential to the successful score as the blend and contrast of pigments in a painting. To pursue the analogy, pictorial art ranges from line drawings to rich and dazzling arrays of colour, so in music the accent may be on linear elements, reducing colour to a minimum as, for instance, a keyboard fugue might prove to be. The gradations leading to intoxicating glories of glowing colour pass through sombre or bright hues. A painting may incorporate features which are austere or cold or dark, other parts of the scheme being vivid, warm and full of light. The skill of the artist lies in his capacity to harmonize these elements, building them into his design—all his judgement and informed experience placing his technique at the disposal of his inspiration and imagination.

In the realm of painting then, skill and artistic insight are brought to bear upon the problem of achieving the desired expression by means of subtle tints, bold splashes or a judicious combination of both. To what degree these shall be used is a question of trained and intuitive judgement. Similarly, in music the orchestrator's judgement suggests the appropriate *means* demanded by his ideas: general medium tones, subtle and changing blends or occasional moments of pure sound from one particular group or family.

Pure tones can be an important factor in scoring. Although the majority of scores do not seem to indulge in stretches of such colour for long periods, the brief periods in which they occur are often chosen to be striking and arresting (not necessarily exciting). Contrasts of pure colour are bold and unmistakable:

Example 25   Bar by bar colour contrasts   *The Undaunted* (Eric Ball)
              (also contrast of tensions)

A background of contrasted colour throwing a melody line into relief (see also Examples 8 and 100a):

Example 26   *Themes from the 'New World' symphony* (Dvořák, arr R. S.-A.)
(F.S 274)

(Original: Cor anglais with string background)

Alternations of pure colour which occur too frequently are apt to be fussy. This generalized observation does not include the contrast of large and small groups in works of a *concertante* nature. No doubt carefully designed exploitation in skilful hands could brilliantly prove the comment wrong—but the comment is made as a word of caution. It is borne out by examination of the scores referred to in the preparation of this book; more subtle shades are generally employed which allow for the predominance of any particular tone colour as desired.

Chapter 2   COLOUR RESOURCE—MIXED TONES

AS previously suggested, the painter's use of subtle tints as well as the bolder hues and intensities has its parallel in instrumentation. Instrumental groups of similar quality (or *timbre*) correspond roughly to the primary, and perhaps secondary colours, but the mixing and harmonious blending of these offer so vast a range of possibilities that the comparatively few examples to be quoted can only touch the fringe. If only for this reason—and there are other excellent reasons—the student is urged to make a first-hand study of scores and seek out for himself the thinking behind the variety of instrumental handling he will encounter therein.

Theoretically, any combination of brass might be regarded as possible, and indeed most instruments will combine reasonably satisfactorily. Whilst occasions arise when one is fortunate enough to be called upon to write for first-rate players, one does not always enjoy the luxury of performance by the ideal band. Certain passages are difficult of attainment and not always effective even when undertaken by the best aggregates. Nerves, extreme register, tuning and instrumental idiosyncrasies are factors, the overlooking or ignoring of which may put the composer or arranger at risk.

On the whole, the plan of this book is to choose examples which illustrate standard practice. On this foundation the imaginative and aware composer will develop his own techniques in the modelling of the plastic material of his personal creative thinking.

In the mixing of tone-colours there may be a neutral blend or the predominance of a colour according to the nature of the parts included and the register in which they are playing.

Doubling at the unison (the duplication of parts is known as doubling). Equal balance, uniting tenor trombones and euphonium.

Example 27   *Torchbearers* (Eric Ball)
(G.S. 1069)

Horns, baritone, trombones—a strong unison line of medium intensity:

Example 28   *Themes from the 'New World' symphony* (Dvořák, arr R. S.-A.)
(F.S. 274)

The addition of euphonium to such a line would greatly enrich it. In the above instance such a degree of richness was not required.

Solo cornets, horns, euphonium—very intense. The sound is somewhat reminiscent of violins playing 'sul G' (the lowest string):

Example 29   *Sound out the proclamation* (Eric Ball)
(G.S. 1098)

A three-octave doubling. The lower octaves are balanced, the upper is not but will be heard, being uppermost. Addition of soprano and flugel or solo cornets would strengthen such a line where needed. In this excerpt the orchestral score has less weight on the upper line:

Example 30   *Themes from the 'New World' symphony* (Dvořák, arr R. S.-A.)
(F.S. 274)

See also Examples 9 and 10

Thirds doubled at the octave:

Example 31   *Themes from the 'New World' symphony* (Dvořák, arr R. S.-A.)
(F.S. 274)

Note the effectiveness and sense of independent *character* when a line is doubled at the octave by a different instrumental colour:

Example 32 *Scena Sinfonica* (Henry Geehl)

It will be evident that the limit is not reached with unison/octave or two-part doubling. If a 'trumpet' family quartet is doubled exactly by a 'saxhorn' quartet eight players will be employed although there are still only four basic parts (ie harmonically). This fact, self-evident though it may be, points the way to fuller ensembles wherein duplication of parts is likely to occur. Reference to Example 19 will illustrate a complete ensemble of cornets and tenor trombones duplicating, in three octaves, a two-part line.

A convenient pair of quartets could be (a) two cornets, tenor trombone and bass trombone, (b) flugel, horn, baritone, euphonium.

If the second quartet group be now changed to replace the flugel by the euphonium as the melody instrument, allocating the bass part to an E♭ bass, the saxhorn quality is retained but the character of the quartet is now that of melody in an inner part. The resulting combination of the quartets begins to resemble that of a small band. (For practical purposes the extra weight of harmony parts might prompt the importing of an extra melody cornet. Or the original quartet with flugel might remain, adding the euphonium as an extra, ie a quintet.)

An illustration of the combined groups retaining flugel:

Example 33 (Concert pitch) *The Coventry Carol*

In this carol the bass trombone plays the upper notes of the bass part. Euphonium doubling of this part would most likely be identical; in transferring the part to the E♭ bass the lower octave is quite often allocated as the bass line is rather high. One could use the B♭ bass and maintain the bass line consistently an octave lower. If fidelity to the *shape* of the bass line can be maintained it is all to the good.

Chapter 3 THE FULL BAND

1 CHORD VOICING

EXAMPLES have been given of scoring for both families of instruments. As the carol arrangement at the end of the preceding chapter illustrated, the two families in combination yield a *tutti*. This *tutti* will vary in sonority and intensity in accordance with the positioning of the various parts. We saw that doubling is almost inevitably in evidence as the score is not intended to be a combination of 16 or 17 independent harmony parts. As will be noted later in the book, duplicating parts do not necessarily double slavishly, furthermore rhythmic patterns and rests create independent instrumental parts although the harmony on which they are based may still be three-, four- or five-part.

The simplest form of *tutti* writing: the chorale or hymn tune should logically appear here. The subject is reserved as a separate consideration (see page 23) and could be read at this point if desired.

High registers are brilliant (a) or intense (b).

Low registers are mellow, sonorous, and/or solid according to the dynamic (c) and (d).

Because of the overtones it is not necessary to fill up the upper harmony by high cornets (d). It is sometimes done, of course, to add the brilliance of upper register: soprano and *divisi* solo cornets (e). See also the note about four-foot addition at the end of Chapter 4.

Example 34

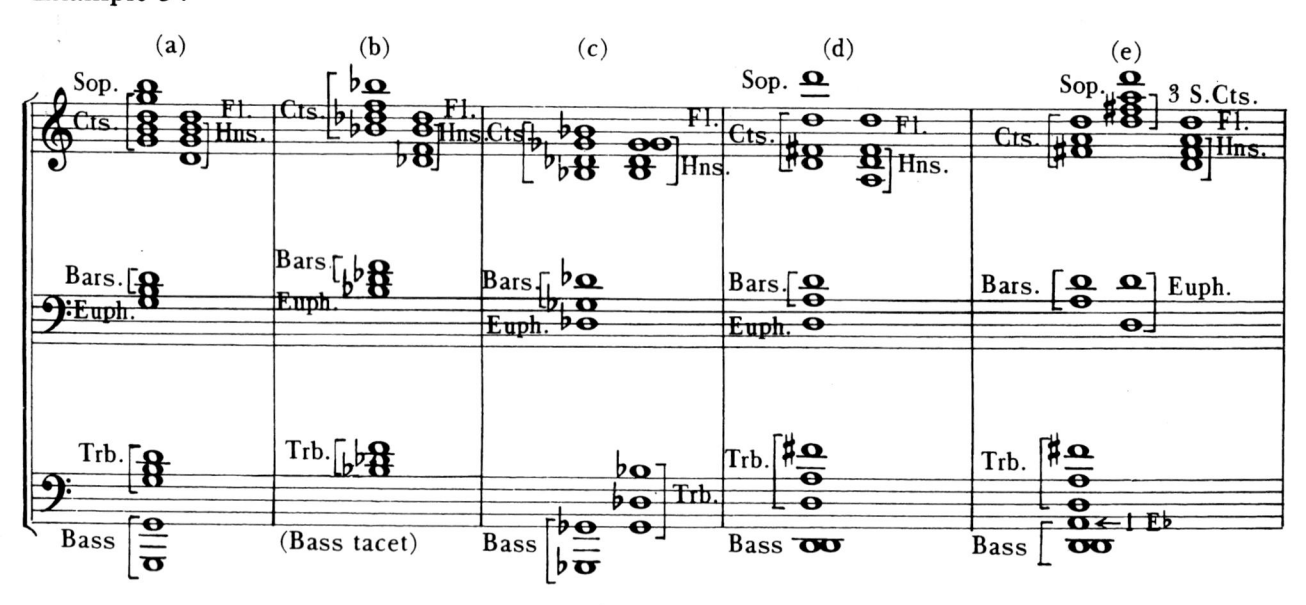

Example 6 drew attention to the brilliance of high trombones *fortissimo*. Positioned closely in the upper-medium to upper register they add this quality and 'bite' to a chord of which they are a component: see (a) and (b) above. Of these two chords the 'middle' of (a) would be somewhat more rich. 'Open' scoring, as in (c), (d) and (e), adds a fullness which becomes more rich as the register deepens, as at (c).

As in vocal or orchestral layouts, the normal procedure is to widen the gap between parts as they become lower. Thick and low chords tend to be 'muddy'. Unless the chord lies very low it is seldom that one encounters the third of the chord written lower than E or D for baritone, trombone or euphonium.

Some writers like to introduce low fifths; these are warm and rich, especially in seventh chords or their multiples.

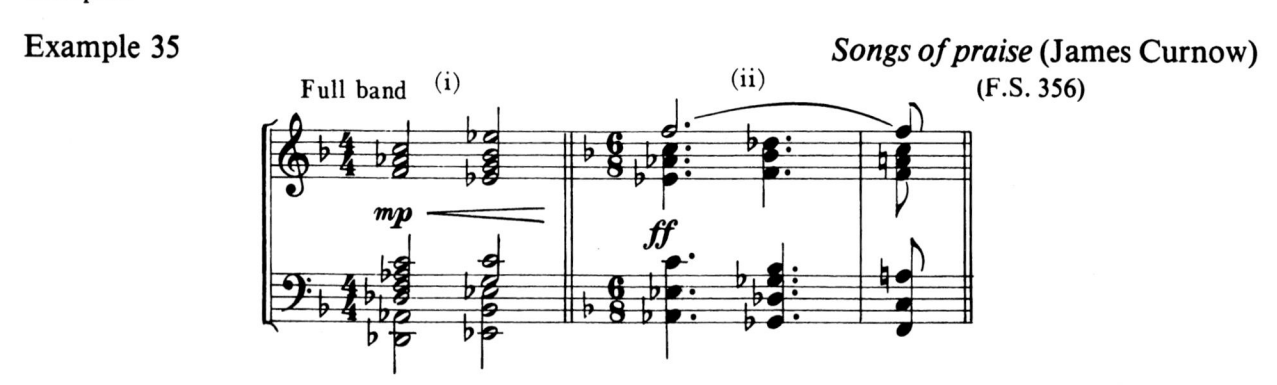

Example 35   *Songs of praise* (James Curnow)
                                                            (F.S. 356)

If indulged too freely, the effectiveness soon palls. Usually the E♭ basses are divided; sometimes the upper E♭ bass is doubled by the lower of divided euphoniums. The thick sonorities, like other striking devices, tend to lose their effectiveness if over-exploited.

2 THE *TUTTI*

When the full complement of instruments is employed, it is an old maxim that each group (eg horns or trombones) should be as harmonically complete as possible, ensuring a satisfactory balance of parts. Identical doubling of certain parts as, for instance, 2nd horn and 1st baritone for page after page, is not regarded as ideal and an inspection of first-rate scores reveals differences wholesale or subtle. The development of a composition will naturally dictate the instruments to be employed at any given time: sometimes whole groups will retain family identity for a number of pages, at other times the music is more broken up into individual excursions and contributions. We are considering the use of the complete band and it would be hopeless to attempt to summarize extensive practice into a few 'rules'. What we shall do is to examine typical handling in a methodical manner and analyse points therein illustrated.

A few bars of typical *tutti* at a *fortissimo* climax:

Example 36   *Scena Sinfonica* (Henry Geehl)

A strong melodic line is provided by soprano, solo cornet, repiano and euphonium. Toward the end of bar three the range becomes rather too high for repiano and it drops to a harmony part; the strength of line is maintained as the 3rd cornet now has the melody in unison with the euphonium. The supporting parts are laid out to secure maximum richness, the trombones being in a medium register where their sonority and 'edge' is telling. In bar two the bass trombone adds depth, whereas the E♭ bass is in a fairly high register, intensifying the bass line. At one point the 2nd baritone and 2nd trombone double the bass (bar 2), which is a useful addition to reinforce the basses in an upper register when the euphonium is otherwise engaged. It will be observed that both trumpet and saxhorn families make complete and satisfactory harmony with the bass.

A passage demonstrating the build-up and dissipation of a climax:

Example 37
The Kingdom Triumphant (Eric Ball)
(F.S. 273)

There are some sharp extremes of volume. In the work this is a dramatic sequence, ultimately leading to the final, broad theme. Note first the attack of the *fortissimo* timpani roll on the otherwise silent second beat of the first 3/2 bar. Brilliance is added to the leap of the horns by the upper-octave soprano. The *fortissimo-piano* has its dramatic effect, once in the horn/soprano figure, answered—again on the second beat—by lower-range instruments in a solid and resonant medium/low register. The high horn sound stands well out over the thick low chord—one is aware of the trombone 'edge'. As this chord-colour dies away the cornets 'grow' through it so that, at the second bar of the 4/2, the cornet sound is partially supreme. The lower chord is also increasing—trombones have moved into a higher register, especially the 1st trombone now really identifying with the lower 2nd cornet. Top and bottom parts now move outwards, creating a feeling of expansion; the *riten* adds its degree of breadth.

The climax is reached and begins to relax (a) by reduction of volume, (b) by reduction of instrumental tension, most of the parts dropping to lower notes. Soprano and flugel are withdrawn.

Some scores now are using the four solo cornets as separate entities, with a two-stave part.

Chapter 4 STANDARD FULL BAND LAY-OUT OF A HYMN TUNE

EXCELLENT advice has been given in other books on the scoring of hymn tunes—that by the late Dr Harold Hind being, regrettably, now out of print. In some ways the fundamental approach has quite a strong influence over the handling of the band *tutti* in more complex work. The author regards it as probable that among his readers will be those desirous of developing arranging skill and this is sufficient reason for including so 'plain-Jane' a matter with material more creatively glamorous.

Certain principles have already been stated and implied. The combination of two quartet families pointed toward the involvement of all the instruments of the band.

The general plan is straightforward. It is the transfer of the four vocal parts to the brass (most hymns being four-part versions).

1 TRANSPOSITION

It has been assumed that facts about the pitch of brass band instruments are known, also that with one exception (excluding percussion) they use the treble clef. Readers will hardly have arrived thus far without this situation being evident. In order to align with the pitch of the tune being transcribed, the written pitch of the B flat instrument must be raised a tone. Transpositions for E flat instruments are a consequence.

There are two observations to be made at this stage:
(i) Practicality may indicate a transposition of a semitone should an extreme key be otherwise created (as, for instance, a tune pitched in A). One would, of course, ensure that other considerations, such as organ involvement, were not overlooked.
(ii) One might not even trouble to transpose at all, especially if the original hymn is pitched rather high, as is the case with some older hymnals. If one is scoring for congregational singing a concert E or E♭ is high enough for comfort.

2 ALLOCATION OF SOME BASIC PARTS

The ensuring of adequate instrumentation proposes the allotting of vocal lines to 'safe' parts. Thus:

Vocal	*Brass* (a)	(b)
soprano	solo/repiano (1st) cornet	solo/repiano (1st) cornet
alto	2nd cornet, 1st horn	2nd cornet, solo horn
tenor	2nd horn, 1st baritone	1st horn, 1st baritone
bass	basses E♭ and B♭	basses E♭ and B♭

Scheme (a) the standard pattern for SA hymns—recognizes the average working register of the 1st and 2nd horn and leaves the solo horn free to double the alto (see notes below) or fulfil a freelance role. The scheme may have developed from the instrumentation of the SA's journal for smaller and young bands, having 1st and 2nd horn only.

Scheme (b) ensures a stronger tenor representation. Additionally it allows for the fact that some bands might not dispense with solo horn in favour of 2nd horn; in a very small group this could be a harmonic disaster!

3 ALLOCATION OF REMAINING PARTS

Soprano

Almost invariably the soprano has the melody line in unison with the cornets or at the octave. Ideally, maintain a coherent linear part, especially during the course of a phrase.

Flugel

Frequently doubles the melody. A wide space between soprano and alto can be filled up by flugel and/or solo horn. Both flugel and solo horn can be employed to reinforce the alto.

Solo horn

This is a remaining part only in terms of scheme (a). Even then it will largely play the alto part. See also comment under 'flugel'.

2nd Baritone

The value of this part is not always appreciated or even understood. In hymn tune scoring it generally follows the tenor line. However, one is thinking practically and tends to regard the 2nd baritone as having a rather more limited range in work designed for the less advanced group. Hence the preparation of a tune book dictates an upper limit of about C or D. As the solo horn is useful for thickening the harmony (when appropriate) so the 2nd baritone fulfils three roles; (a) doubles 1st baritone when the tenor line is in a medium register and may lose the resonance necessary for adequate balance, (b) duplicates other harmony notes when the tenor rises too high, thus enriching the texture, (c) doubles a bass line or selected notes (rather rare but can be useful). It must be emphasized that the part should not dodge about but have a coherent linear shape.

Euphonium

Some older hymn tune arrangements used to delight in florid euphonium parts. These are largely, if not altogether, *passé,* although a strong tune can be enhanced by a contrapuntal line or phrase of character. The two mainstream uses of euphonium are to play the melody or the bass. Melody allocation is useful to give a change of colour, the melody cornets being directed to rest for a verse. A high vocal bass normally implies euphonium, otherwise there is a wide gap, the high bass obviously having a higher tenor above it. The bass section will double at the octave, unless an eight-foot effect is desired. This may be an appropriate point at which to mention the value of the four-part basic schemes which permit various permutations of instruments.

Trombones

This group has rather special consideration. The ideal is that they be present as a trio. In some arrangements their usefulness as a colour element leads to the complete group having occasional rests for complete phrases. The practicality of this approach in a functional situation may be arguable.

There are two standard ways of using the tenor trombones as harmony parts (whilst the following may be slightly over-simplified it is a workable guide, dictated by musical judgement in a particular situation):

(i) 1st trombone—alto (doubling 2nd cornet)
     2nd trombone—tenor (doubling 1st baritone);
(ii) 1st trombone—tenor
     2nd trombone—other harmony notes (perhaps similar to 2nd baritone)—even melody.

Situations (i) and (ii) are dictated by the height of the tenor part. It may be that the parts will be a mixture of both schemes: where the 1st trombone takes the alto the 2nd trombone will play the tenor. At some point the 1st trombone may switch to the tenor (especially where the vocal part is high), the 2nd trombone filling in below, possibly doubling the alto an octave lower. The part writing should be directionally logical and not aimless. (NB: It is often the tenor line which, in hymn arrangement, tends to be weaker than the alto. The allocation of both trombones to the tenor line might be considered.)

Some hymns are of a 'unison' type eg 'Sine Nomine' ('For all the saints'), verses 1-3, 7 and 8. The doubling of the tune by the tenor trombones (and perhaps also the euphonium) is satisfying and strong.

Bass trombone

Lends sonority to the bass line in its lower register. However the sense of compactness ought to be maintained by a consideration of the trombone section as a group. Earlier comments regarding the use of trombones in the band will be valid in terms of the above generalizations.

A scoring of 'St Cecilia' will illustrate the above.

Example 38 *St Cecilia*

(a) Soprano and alto are unison; solo horn fills up chord.
(b) Chord filling, avoiding doubled leading note.
(c) Completing triad as bass trombone has tonic.
(d) 1st trombone switches from alto to tenor; 2nd trombone takes over tenor.
(e) When 1st trombone plays two alto notes 2nd trombone plays the two tenor notes.
(f) Tonic chosen as the 3rd is in the bass.
(g) Low dominant thickens chord.
(h) S.A. scoring often gives the melody line in small notes.

A four-foot addition

In some scores the soprano, repiano and flugel are treated as an independent trio, taking into account the fact that these three players often sit next to one another. The varying colours of the three instruments blend well, and can often 'top' the lower harmonies with good effect, sometimes adding four-foot effects to the basic eight-foot, as in the organ.

Chapter 5 THE *TUTTI*

1 CHORAL SCORING

IN discussing the saxhorn family reference was made, in terms of range, to the approximate vocal equivalents of brass.

'Choral' scoring occurs when the instrumentation is planned on a broad four- or five-part basis, the parts being allocated in accordance with their general pitch level.

Example 39   *'Neath Italian skies* (R. S.-A.)
                                                                              (G.S. 1427)

The arrangement is clearly defined:
    (a) Melody — upper cornets and tenor trombones
    (b) Alto   — 2nd cornet, flugel and horns
    (c) Tenor   — Baritones and euphonium
    (d) Bass   — Bass trombone and basses.

The writer owes a debt to Eric Ball, something of a parallel scheme being used by him at an earlier date (1938).

(Example 40)

Example 40   *The Pilgrim Way* (Eric Ball)
(G.S. 1138)

The grouping in the above example is:
- (a) Melody — upper cornets and flugel
- (b) Alto — 2nd cornet and horns
- (c) Tenor — Baritones, tenor trombones and upper euphonium
- (d) Bass — Lower euphonium, bass trombone and basses.

2 THE *TUTTI*—GROUP SCORING

Group scoring denotes the allocation of distinctive features to individual sections of the band, the various sections being employed more or less simultaneously to create the *tutti*. Erik Leidzén's festival march 'Following the Flag' provides a clear example.

Example 41   *Following the flag* (Erik Leidzén)
(F.S. 181)

Three groups are combined:
- (i) cornets and trombones
- (ii) flugel and horns
- (iii) baritones, euphoniums and basses.

3 THE SMALL BAND

In the educational field graded and teaching books have recognized the needs of beginning bands. The instrumentation as well as technical difficulty has been kept minimal. As such books are functional they tend to justify their existence on the basis of the provision of music which is fairly easy; the simple arrangements are therefore less concerned with colour, although the element is not ignored in the more progressive essays.

Consideration to music for smaller bands was given by The Salvation Army in the USA around 1936. This may well have been influenced by Scandinavian ideas, for the Norwegians had used a six-piece ensemble for decades and Sweden published a regular journal for E♭ soprano, solo cornet, 1st and 2nd cornet, three horns, baritone, two tenor trombones, euphonium, basses and percussion.

From the Salvationist Music Department in New York came, in 1947, a publication relying largely on cornets and trombones, high school bands producing more players of these instruments than of the horn type. The effect is quite bright and sparkling, the scheme being: a basic group—

3 cornets   (1st frequently *divisi* and 2nd)
2 E*b* horns
2 tenor trombones
euphonium
basses
percussion.

Soprano, baritone (one), and bass trombone are optional extras.

The British solution arose from the method followed in its tune book production of 1952—on the lines outlined previously. The *Unity Series,* as it was called, first appeared in 1958, the editor being Colonel Albert Jakeway. In this lay-out a four-part system was adopted:

1st cornet
2nd cornet—1st horn
2nd horn—baritone or trombone (one)
basses
optional euphonium.

This arrangement has been influential in succeeding productions by other publishers.

An earlier Salvationist editor, Colonel Frederick Hawkes, brought into being, in 1921, a journal series he called *Second Series* (now *Triumph Series*). This dispenses with solo cornet, flugel and solo horn. Occasionally, however, the 2nd cornet part is marked 'flugel' where, if available, a flugel is desirable for a particular passage.

The foregoing references are indicative of the general approach and no apology is felt to be necessary for quoting the lines of development as relating to a movement which has played a large part in pioneering small-band publication—rendered necessary for functional reasons.

That the practical needs of young players are ever under consideration is illustrated by recent advertising of new books of hymn tunes and arrangements for schools having some parts specifically designed for very elementary standards of attainment. In some publications the piano is included as a support.

Chapter 6 GENERAL ENSEMBLES

SOME of the matter in this section is applicable to considerations of texture because under this head are combinations which are not entirely *tutti* nor restricted to a single melodic line. Whilst there are many pieces which keep the full band employed practically throughout, these are not usually highly developed works. Apart from the *music* content—the play of ideas—the light and shade of a sound-picture will be closely related to the interchange and variety of instrumentation, with grades in between the *tutti* and the fine line-drawing of a solo *motif*. One notices, throughout the unfolding of a score, the fluidity of entry and exit of parts, sometimes alone, often in consort. To change the metaphor to that of the stage, the action may involve the whole cast, a dialogue or soliloquy and so on. The interaction of the characters, plot (if any), language, evocation of atmosphere, crises, climaxes, rise and fall of emotion, timing and pace of action or speech are all the ingredients which go to make up the hour or two of involvement with the players which is the experience of playgoing. The musical parallel needs no spelling out. There can be no hard and fast rules, only examinations of typical situations.

Example 42   *Entertainments* (Gilbert Vinter)

This passage from the Elegy has a dual melodic line, for solo cornet and euphonium, supported by a pulsating group of horns with sustained bass. The general level is low-key. In the third bar the single lines become double duet; added instruments thicken the texture and, as the *crescendo* operates, the horns rise to a more penetrating and intense register.

Example 43

Victory (R. S.-A.)
(F.S. 237)

A cornet and trombone group accompanied thinly by two horns and basses. The euphonium has an undulating figure which keeps the movement 'alive'.

Example 44   *Resurgam* (Eric Ball)
(F.S. 302)

Antiphonal groups (a) horns and euphonium in octaves, (b) baritones and basses in tenths. Where the baritones join the horns (a third lower) the addition of trombones makes a satisfactory blend and balance.

Example 45   *Suite in Bb* (Purcell—Geehl)

An instructive excerpt showing a scoring of Purcell's music first for full band and then thinning out to a much lighter ensemble:

Example 46   *I know a Fount* (Thomas Rive)
                                                              (F.S. 238)

The first of a set of variations on the above song-theme passes the melodic line between solo cornet, flugel and solo horn in the following order: horn—flugel—horn—cornet—horn—flugel—cornet—flugel—cornet—flugel. A feature of this composer's style is the subtle manipulation of suspensions so that the harmony does not come to rest until the desired cadence is reached.

33

Example 47   *Rhapsody in Brass* (Dean Goffin)

[musical score: Soprano Eb, Solo Cornet Bb, Flugel Bb, Solo Horn Eb, 1st Horn Eb, 2nd Horn Eb, 1st Baritone Bb, 2nd Baritone Bb, Euphonium Bb, Eb Bass, Bb Bass]

A section in the course of thematic discussion. Little need be said about these bars, but observe how the colours are changed and that the composer marshalls his forces so that he has a new set of parts waiting and ready for their entry. Note too how the E♭ bass solo moves smoothly to become a part of the supporting harmony and how the soprano, two bars later, fulfils a similar role. The dynamics are a model: the E♭ bass begins with a comparatively high degree of strength but reduces as it approaches its chord function. The soprano and flugel solos are both a little louder than the supporting chords; the soprano does not reduce by degrees but drops immediately to *pianissimo*.

Example 48   *Resurgam* (Eric Ball)
                                                                              (F.S. 302)

A sound of high intensity created by upper-register scoring and omission of bass trombone and basses:

[musical score: Poco allegro ed agitato; Sop., Cts.; 1st Trb.; Fl., Hns.; Bars.; 2nd Trb., Euph.]

Example 49   *Prometheus Unbound* (Granville Bantock)

In contrast to the foregoing example, this excerpt has a brassy and solid sonority:

Chapter 7   SOLO PASSAGES

1   SOLO PASSAGES

SHORT imitative passages come off well between instruments of contrasted tone quality. In imitative work linear considerations can be more important than colour.

Example 50   *The Valiant Heart* (Philip Catelinet)
                                                                                                   (F.S. 147)

2 BACKGROUNDS TO SOLOS

Backgrounds or accompaniments are planned to allow the soloist to be heard clearly without having to force his sound. Typical accompaniments illustrate this ideal.

(a) A light, open accompaniment:

Example 51 *Trumpet Concerto* (Hummel, arr Vernon Post) (F.S. 330)

(b) A background of contrasted tone-colour; euphonium supported by three trombones, the addition of the B♭ bass adding depth:

Example 52 *The Triumph of Peace* (Eric Ball) (F.S. 130)

(c) A neutral backing. Horn, baritone, euphonium and B♭ bass make a homogeneous blend of similar colour. Note the lay-out of parts where the trombones enter: solo horn as uppermost harmony part, euphonium dovetailed between 1st and 2nd trombones. Strictly speaking this arrangement is rather more of a brass choir type; the preponderance of quaver movement and general independent character of the flugel does, however, create the impression of a solo placed above steadily-paced chord movement, an impression heightened by the *legato* style of these parts.

Example 53 *Norwegian folk songs* (Erik Silfverberg)

An example could not readily be found of accompaniments by instruments of a similar colour, differently employed so as to allow the soloist to stand out (on the lines of Example 53). A word-illustration suggests the possibilities: a *cantabile* solo line surrounded by, or over a tracery of figurations.

Chapter 8   MELODIC LINES

1 MELODIC STRANDS

VARIOUS combinations of instruments at the unison or octave have been examined. Such melodic strands, whether of pure or mixed colour, are to be found in every score. 'Melodic' need not imply a tune but includes a phrase or figure.

In full-band work, when upper cornets have the main stream of a melody, the euphonium, trombone and, occasionally, the baritone are sometimes to be found doubling at the octave. Octave doubling often occurs between similar colours, eg cornet and trombone (singular or in group). The effect of doubling can be heightened where the two levels of melodic line differ in colour. The context and effect desired will obviously dictate choice.

See Examples 9, 10, 27-30, 32, 54, 58 and 62 for examples of 'unison' writing.

Eric Ball evokes a medieval atmosphere by using baritones and tenor trombones to 'chant' his original modal setting of John Bunyan's 'Pilgrim Song' ('He who would valiant be'). Were the fullness of the euphonium to be added, it would fatten the colour and render too warm the rather lugubrious monkish character.

Example 54 *The Pilgrim Way* (Eric Ball)
(G.S. 1138)

2 INNER MELODIC LINES

By virtue of its position, an inner melody can fail to achieve requisite prominence if the appropriate problems of balance are not solved. Considerations of *weight* (number of instruments employed), *volume* and *intensity* (penetrating register or otherwise) in relation to what else is going on will be judged to produce the desired proportion of importance in the scheme.

The simplest illustration is that of the familiar march counter-melody, allocated to euphonium and baritones, rather less often to euphonium and tenor trombones, quite frequently to euphonium, baritones and tenor trombones.

If not heavily outweighed, movement in an inner part has a good chance of coming through sustained chords. In the following example, against the static chord (reducing in volume) the movement of the euphonium enables the solo passage to penetrate:

Example 55

Song of courage (Eric Ball)
(F.S. 258)

Example 56

Minuet from 'The Severn Suite' (Edward Elgar)

The light and open texture is marked much quieter than the baritone melody.

Example 57

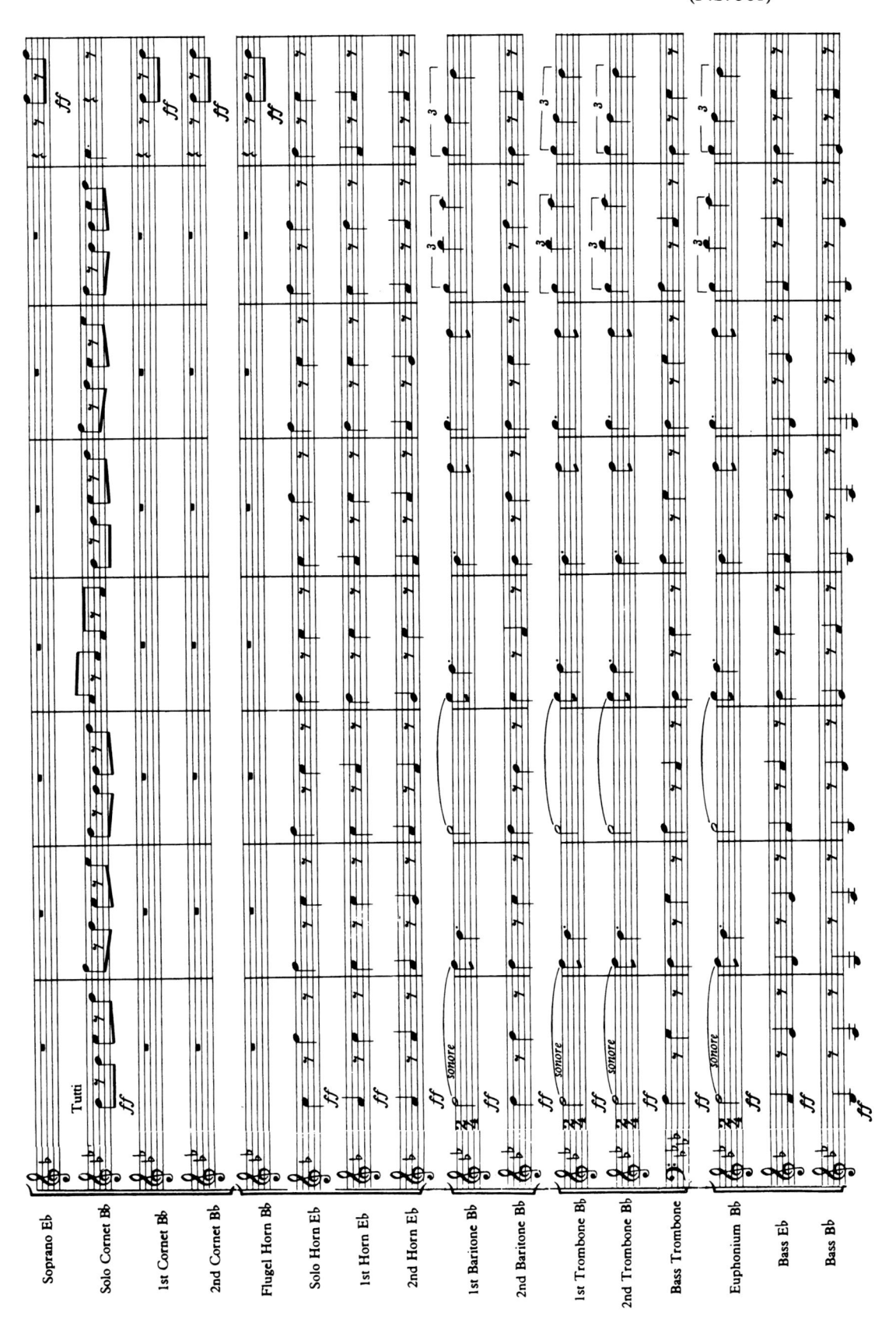

I saw three ships (Brian Bowen)
(F.S. 361)

The strong, expansive line comes through intensely against the tripping quavers of the carol and the steady tread of the accompaniment. Earlier in the work this is a theme in its own right; a climactic passage is created by combining it (in augmentation) with the carol subject.

A rich inner voice, useful in main-line or in an imitative capacity, is created by blending tenor trombones with euphonium:

Example 58   *The Warrior Psalm* (R. S.-A)
(F.S. 358)

*Bass trombone reinforces the low E in this bar then joins basses.

3 REINFORCED PHRASE OR FIGURE

Perhaps a portion of a melody, or a significant phrase or *motif,* requires emphasis. The addition of an extra instrument, or instruments, at this point achieves the end effectively.

Example 59   *Variations for brass band* (R. Vaughan Williams)

An inner melody on lower cornets, first and second horns is brought into greater prominence by the addition of trombones, even though the first horn moves off to another part.

Example 60   *The Eternal Presence* (Eric Ball)
                                                                    (F.S. 314)

The horn unison, plus a cornet or two, is sufficiently prominent when punctuated by a light group. In the fourth bar soprano, lower cornets and trombones are providing a solid block of sound and the solo cornets are moving to the upper octave. Flugel and baritones add the necessary weight to enable the lower line to hold its own.

4 RANGE-LIMIT

One of the frustrations of writing for brass band is that of range-limit. Compositionally the limitation is a discipline. At times a part goes out of range.

Example 61   *The call of the righteous* (Leslie Condon)
                                                                    (F.S. 294)

Whilst theoretically the whole passage is possible on the flugel, it would require the technique of a virtuoso to achieve it. Practical considerations therefore have dictated the taking over of the high notes by the soprano. The somewhat sharper sound of the soprano also lends a touch of brilliance. Two bars later the passage is similarly shared between B*b* and E*b* bass (cf Example 20—basses).

The extension of the E♭ bass by baritones, the euphonium playing the whole figure.

Example 62   *Rhapsody in Brass* (Dean Goffin)

5 OVERLAPPING

Unless for special reasons it is normally desirable where possible to continue a phrase by means of an instrument (instruments) of similar colour. *The overlapping of parts* ensures a smooth continuity (see above examples). In the example below the line could have been taken up by trombones but horns were chosen (a) for increased mellowness (b) for relaxed middle register. Note the overlap:

Example 63   *Themes from the 'New World' symphony* (Dvořák, arr R. S.-A.)
                                                                    (F.S. 274)

The continuity mentioned above is a regular instrumentation practice. In the long span of music from which an extract is quoted, range and breathing are facilitated by overlapping and taking over (Example 64):

Example 64 — *A Kensington Concerto* (Eric Ball)

The following illustrates a means of sustaining a pedal.

Example 65 — *Joan of Arc* (Denis Wright)

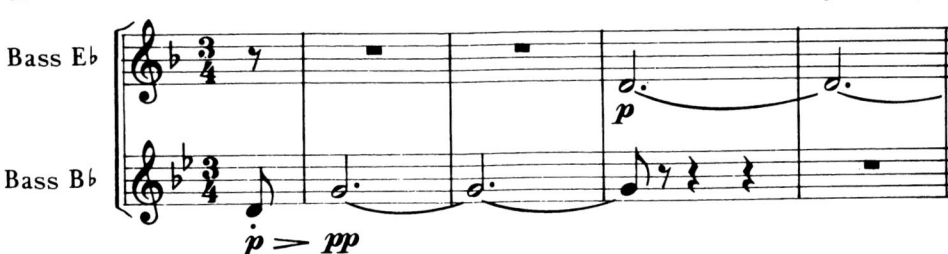

As the E♭ bass begins his held note the trombones enter with a thematic statement, the added weight of which doubtless suggested the increases of the pedal dynamic.

SUSTAINED BINDING TONES

(a) *Holding note or counter-melody*

A rhythmic accompaniment of the vamp type is inclined to sound brittle if the melody is of a jerky character. The use of single holding note of counter-melody helps to 'bind' the music together. Such recourse is commonplace in many a march and quotation is unnecessary. Whilst on this point there is a good deal to be said for aiming for a satisfying degree of harmonic completeness in the three strands: theme, counter-melody and bass. Counter-melodies will be referred to under 'textures'. Both this note and the one which follows are relevant to the subject of texture.

(b) *Sustained harmonics*

The idea of a holding note is usefully extended to chordal blocks which perform a similar function (in this example, the trombones).

Example 66   *Eine kleine nachtmusik* (Mozart, arr A. H. Jakeway) (F.S. 210)

This is, of course, an added dimension to the original string composition, but is an excellent illustration.

Chapter 9   SPECIAL EFFECTS

THE nature of an instrument, its construction and manner of handling, including the various ways in which sounds can be produced, are its *characteristics,* the features of which are capable of being effectively exploited for the composer's or arranger's purposes: for instance, the strummed chords of a guitar or the *pizzicati* of strings. These characteristics may well influence the concepts being formulated by creative activity, eg the possibility of piano *arpeggi* particularly leads to a certain style of keyboard writing when compared with, say, the organ where sustaining qualities and stops offer different possibilities. Whilst both instruments have much in common in the sense of struck chords and contrapuntal lines, one is percussive and the dissolving sounds only create an illusion of sustained line, whereas the other's continuity is actual. The piano however is delicately flexible as to *nuance* and fluctuation depending on touch; organ technique approaches these considerations in a different way.

Basically all brass instruments are played in a similar manner, ie the air in the tube is set in motion by lip vibration and a stream of air through a mouthpiece. The valve instruments have pre-set tube lengths altered by valve permutation, whereas the trombones change tube length by movement of a slide. An extremely virtuoso level of rapidity can be obtained on the trombone but obviously the facility of valves is superior to the comparative distances a trombone slide must cover. The trombone, however, is capable of a true *glissando* (so long as the required slide movements permit). Other than this particular feature, which will be mentioned in due course, the characteristics discussed in this chapter are held in common by brass instruments but are not exclusive to them. Such effects abound in scores of all kinds although the method by which they are produced will vary as for instance the tremolo: produced by string fingering in a different manner than, say, a cornet using valve alternations or lipped harmonics.

1 SIMULATED *PIZZICATO*

The nearest approach is *staccato* and an approximation of a *pizzicato* bass can be effectively produced. Vaughan Williams uses the device and simultaneously sustains the part by one E♭ bass.

Example 67 *Prelude on three Welsh hymn tunes* (R. Vaughan Williams)
(F.S. 209)

2 POINTED CHORDS

Sometimes colloquially known as 'shot notes', the use of the full band on an attacked crotchet or quaver is striking.

Example 68

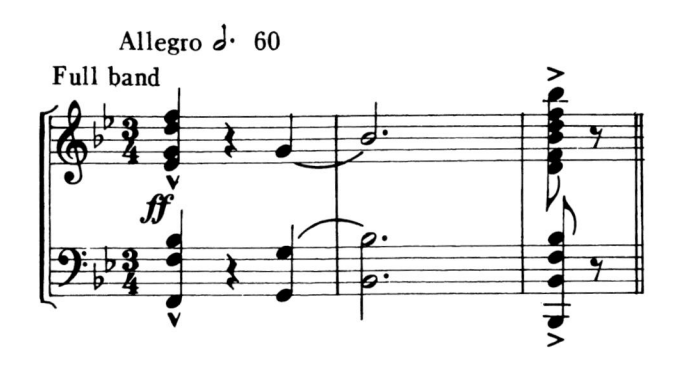

3 FORTE-PIANO

A loud attack followed immediately by a decrease in volume.

Example 69 *New Frontier* (William Himes)
(F.S. 365)

Example 70

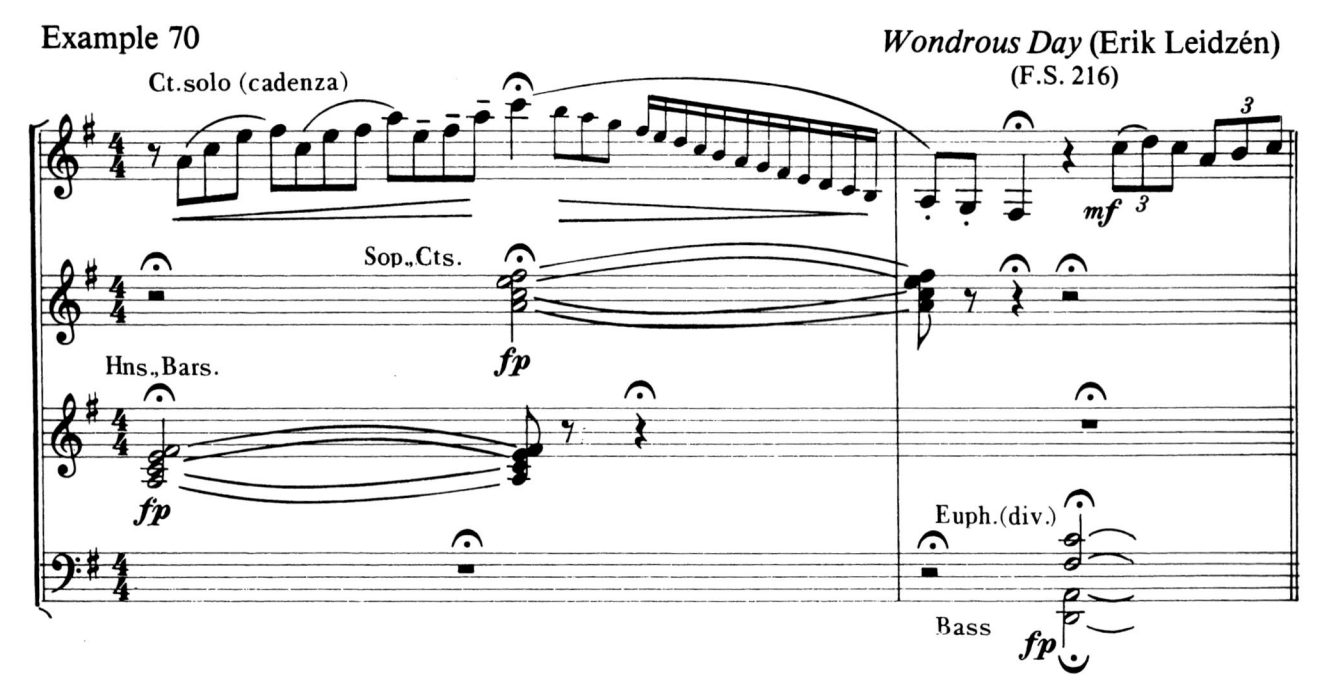

Wondrous Day (Erik Leidzén)
(F.S. 216)

Instances are found of a small group sustaining the chord after the main ensemble has ceased; this 'cut-off' sharply and strikingly points up the total effect:

Example 71

The Conqueror (R. S.-A.)
(F.S. 292)

4 GLISSANDO

Secured by rapid movement of the trombone slide without articulation, and frequently leading to a principal note. A short *glissando,* of about a semitone, as an *acciaccatura* artistically used, is a regular part of trombone stock-in-trade in jazz contexts. The full slide movement can degenerate into a vulgar, cheap effect (which may be required for a particular reason, of course). Occasionally the use may relate to a specific extra-musical idea; Charles Skinner secures a 'lion roar' by means of four trombones:

Example 72

Heroes of the faith (Charles Skinner)
(F.S. 170)

It is not unusual to give the shifts.

Under this heading comes the 'smear' and other effects, for a long time exclusive, or almost so, to jazz musicians, but—like other influences from the jazz world—encountered from time to time in brass band scores.

5 RIP

A transfer from the orchestral horn, the term is practically self-explanatory. The player 'rips' into a high note from a relatively low one; the effect has something of the hunting horn about it.

Example 73 *Saints of God* (James Curnow)
(F.S. 388)

6 LIP TRILL

(Trills are normally obtainable from rapid alternations of valves.) The lip trill is usually high in the register where the harmonics are closer together. As a rule lip trills are featured in trombone writing (the slide is unsuitable, making rapid trilling inelegant), but other parts are written.

Example 74 *Just like John* (Norman Bearcroft)
(F.S. 360)

7 LIP ARPEGGIO (more accurately LIPPED ARPEGGIO)

A development of the faculty of passing from one note to another of a harmonic series by means of increased lip tension (ascending) and relaxation (descending).

Example 75 *Concertino for band and trombone* (Erik Leidzén)
(F.S. 211)

8 TREMOLO

The rapid alternation of two notes. Obtained either by valve fingering or by the lip if the notes are part of the same harmonic series and require no valve or slide change.

(a)
Example 76 *Song of courage* (Eric Ball)
(F.S. 258)

(b)
Example 77 *Concertino for band and trombone* (Erik Leidzén)
(F.S. 211)

9 ENHARMONIC TREMOLO

The reiteration of one note obtained by the use of alternative fingering. It is written:

Example 78   *The Great Physician* (A. H. Jakeway)
(F.S. 89)

and the fingerings are usually given. There are instances of high cornet *chords* in *Le Roi d'Ys* (Lalo, arr Frank Wright) and *Diadem of Gold* (G. Bailey).

The effect approximates to the reiterated string tremolo on a single note.

10 FLUTTER TONGUING

A method of trilling the tongue and producing a 'burring' effect.

Example 79   *The Present Age* (Leslie Condon)

11 THE 'PYRAMID'

A piling up of successive notes of a chord. Sometimes it is coupled with a 'bell' effect, each entry (subsequently sustained) attacking its note in *martellato* fashion.

Example 80   *The Witness* (William Himes)
(F.S. 335)

To ensure the appearance of each note, the outline is sometimes played, or there is a modified adaptation of both methods.

Where reference has been made to 'chords' this, of course, uses the term loosely to designate any group of simultaneously heard sounds from a simple triad to complex combinations in 'clusters'.

12 AD LIB (RANDOM)

In the traditional mould but very much aware of current trends is Brian Bowen's 'The Day of the Spiritual'. Having built to a high climax-peak of excitement, the composer wishes to dissolve the music by rapid relaxation. His note to the players is to play a given group of notes at will.

Example 81   *The day of the spiritual* (Brian Bowen)

13 MUTES

Mutes have not been exploited in the brass band to the same extent they have in jazz realms. There is room for development and experiment, but as muting is comparatively rare the economics would tend to preclude many slender-budgeted bands from purchasing fresh sets just for the odd occasion. Hence, when muting is asked for it usually turns out to be the straight mute, which is rather nasal and bizarre—ideal for 'cheeky' passages but lacking the rounded warmth for sustained passages. Here the cup mute is preferable, when a remote, yet full concerted sound is obtained. As a rule, muting is for trombones and cornets although there is an example of full-band muting in Elgar's 'Severn Suite'.

When writing for muted instruments the matter of balance needs to be judged; it may be that the muted parts should be marked at a higher degree to ensure audibility, depending on whatever is going on at the time and what, and/or how many unmuted instruments are involved. On the other hand, players are so used to hearing themselves that a passage intended to be, say, a practically inaudible 'cloud' of clustered notes moving through or against other unmuted parts has been known to be overblown to insist on its 'presence'. The conductor could have problems if the calculations are not carefully made and the intention clearly indicated by the composer.

Example 82   *On Ratcliff Highway* (R. S.-A.)

Whilst the Italian terms *con sordino* or *senza sordino* are encountered, the general practice with British scores seems to prefer 'muted' and 'open' or 'mute out'. Practice differs too at which point the players are warned: sometimes at the commencement of the passage itself, or, if a bar's rest or more precedes the passage the direction may be placed earlier.

Muting not only modifies the sound, it obviously reduces volume, a factor which must be taken into account. In the following excerpt the melody is allocated to solo cornets, 1st cornets and tenor trombones playing in octaves and muted. The main reason for the muting is to secure a stridently nasal effect; to ensure the line is not swamped by the fairly full accompaniment it is marked *fortissimo,* the rest of the band being *piano*:

Example 83 *The King's Minstrel* (R. S.-A.)
Allegro scherzando ♩ = 112 (F.S. 313)

See also Examples 8 and 85.

Chapter 10 PERCUSSION

WHILST composers regard percussion as a standard resource, the term has had a rather circumscribed connotation for brass band composers, for it is only during the last two or three decades that many bands have supplemented the basic bass and snare drums plus cymbal(s) and triangle.

For years the percussion department was barred from playing with the band in contests, a curious situation seeing that—until very recently—most, if not all, the significant major works arose from being commissioned for contests.

Usually a matter of economics, timpani gradually made their way into band thinking, together with the paraphernalia of blocks, tambourine, chimes, vibraphones and so on. Then there has been borrowing from the music of nationalist cultures such as castanets and marimbas. The importing of jazz idioms required the rhythm drum kit—and with all this the role of, and demand on the percussionist has increased tremendously.

Anyone seeking to study the subject in depth will profit by reading not only orchestration manuals—there are some recent American ones dealing with popular light music arranging—but also the technical literature produced for the development of percussion players. The present chapter highlights a few of the uses of percussion.

1 SNARE DRUM (or Side Drum)

With the snare in place, the sound is light and crisp. When played without snares ('snares off') it sounds a little wooden but provides a pointed rhythm of a dull, thudding nature. Restraint should be exercised in use. Some of the old hymn tune scores, with long rolls, create a feeling of a rain machine, especially on record. On the other hand, a martial air or snappy march theme receives a brisk 'lift' from the figurations of which the instrument is capable.

2 BASS DRUM

The solitary rolling of a bass drum can create a feeling of expectancy or tension. When building to a climax the snare drum sometimes begins a roll and is joined by the bass drum as the excitement mounts.

3 TIMPANI

Tuned percussion, mostly encountered in pairs; the hand-tuned instruments need advance notice for change of note and, unless the music is fairly diatonic or there is adequate time for such changes, they present problems for the arranger who often has to cudgel his wits to evolve an ingenious solution. Such an instance may be found in music of a sequential nature where the tonality moves beyond the relevance of the two sets of notes with no time for change. Hence the chromatic, pedal timpani are to be preferred and these have gained a good deal of ground. A third instrument would often be helpful and the group of three is not without its advocates. Four sizes are made:

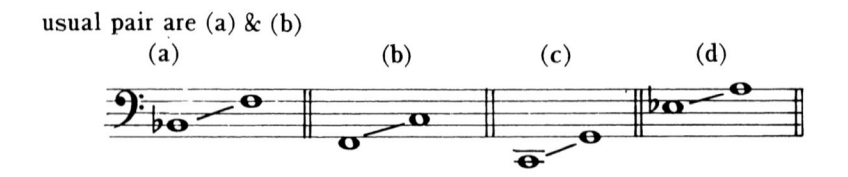

The upper F is more penetrating than the lower octave.

In writing:
(a) The part is written in concert pitch (bass clef).
(b) State the notes first to be set, either by name or on a small stave. Orchestral practice is not consistent. Sometimes the 'tonic' note is given first; sometimes the upper note followed by the lower. With three notes only an inspection of the part may yield the clue.
(c) Indicate the necessary changes as early as possible. Timpani can be muted by placing a piece of felt or soft material on the head. Whilst some scores specify *soft sticks* or *hard sticks* according to a designed effect, in the general way percussionists may reasonably be supposed to have a fair idea of choice of stick head to produce what is intended.

Traditionally the bass and snare drum rolls are shown

whereas the timpani is more often than not written

There is no logic in this but old customs die hard!

Up to the time of writing this book the author has not been aware of timpani writing in chords such as may be encountered with Berlioz. Undoubtedly, the writing of original works for brass band, by composers coming fairly fresh to the medium (whose percussion writing is likely to be more orchestra-orientated) will result in expansion of individual requirements from the band beyond the standard instrumentation. Brass band writers reared in, or closely *au fait* with the medium are, or have been hitherto, disposed to tailor to the standard forces for obvious reasons. Then again a specially-commissioned work—contesting apart—may offer more scope, but even here—as things are at present—a man with his eye on subsequent performances could well feel cautious about indulging himself too luxuriantly in the matter of a battery of percussionists.

On the subject of extra timpani, the writer may perhaps be permitted to make a personal reference to the problem of transcribing two portions of the Berlioz 'Requiem' for band—the choral element being retained for the performance. As may be known, the orchestra in 'Tuba Mirum' requires four separate brass groups (mini-bands) stationed in various parts of the hall. Berlioz uses quite a variety of pitch in his chosen brass instruments but such problems were merely a matter of unravelling and deciding upon suitable brass band equivalents or approximations, ie the normal decisions inherent in any transcription from orchestral to brass band terms.

The point here to be made was that the work calls for 16 timpani which are called upon to play rolls in differing groups producing chords. The chromatic nature of the music allows little or no time for changing. The arranger's problem arose from the fact that bands uniting gave an availability of 10 timpani. The original conception is quite a *tour de force* of percussion writing. The challenge to rival if not exceed Berlioz's own ingenuity was most stimulating but the incident highlights perhaps the writer's conditioning that he accepted the availability of the band timpani—two to each band—rather than thinking of demanding the extras. (In defence there were other factors like space.) Others to come will be less conditioned and it needs no prophetic insight to envisage exotic and unusual groups which still relate loosely to the medium of the brass band.

Additional to their flexibility and capacity for fluent note change, chromatic timpani can produce *glissandi*, the pedal operating whilst the head vibrates.

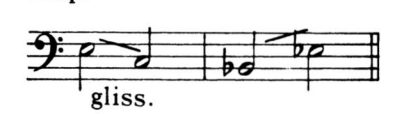

4 CYMBALS

In the brass band the standard is one or more cymbals on stands for striking by a drumstick. The larger have a deep, sonorous resonance. To this group may be added the gong and the clash cymbals—a pair which are struck together. These latter are mostly for big, epic moments.

The cymbal suspended on a stand is usually employed:
(a) solo, at some dramatic or punctuated point;
(b) in a *tutti* at a climax point (cf clash cymbal);
(c) to pick out the rhythmic importance of a part of a bar or passage.

A roll played by bass drum or timpani sticks adds a 'golden' colour to a long note:

Example 84   *The triumph of peace* (Eric Ball)
(F.S. 130)

Or a shimmer:

Example 85   *Song of the eternal* (Leslie Condon)
(F.S. 378)

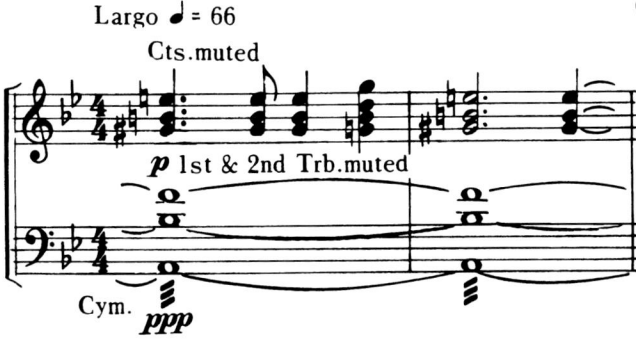

The tremendous effect of a roll played from *pianissimo* through to *fortissimo* is too familiar to need an example.

Hi-hat cymbal: 'rivet cymbal'; such items are familiar impedimenta in the rhythm drum kit. Often the cymbal notation takes the form of diamonds or x's to avoid confusion with the snare drum notes. Cymbals and snare drum are played with brushes as well as sticks.

5 TRIANGLE

Such a dainty instrument as the triangle requires a quiet moment or reduced volume for its note to make any impact. The silvery point it gives to a sounded note is delightful, but quickly loses its fresh attractiveness if overdone. The writer knows of only one instance of a tremolo for triangle; played with a quiet chord it is not too successful.

6 TAMBOURINE

The tambourine evokes Mediterranean or gipsy associations. It is struck, jingled or rolled by rubbing the wet thumb across the parchment. In the latter case show as a *tremolando*.

7 XYLOPHONE, GLOCKENSPIEL AND VIBRAPHONE

Decorative instruments, these are rarely to be met in brass band scores but are increasing in use. The *xylophone* is a popular solo instrument and can be additionally used with hard mallets to give an octave doubling to a cornet melody; this adds brilliance. Point can be given to a biting brass figure. It sounds an octave higher than written.

Glockenspiel: The bell-like sound provides a beautiful decorative colour. The sound is two octaves above that which is written.

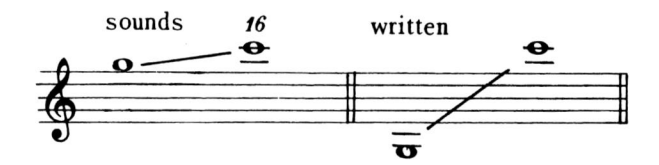

Vibraphone: The instrument is melodic and capable of much more than bell effects and *arpeggi*. Usually two mallets are used but three- or four-note chords can be played. Tubes allow the notes to linger; the sound is dampened by means of a pedal.

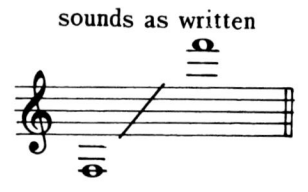

8 CELESTE

A keyboard instrument capable of playing chords.

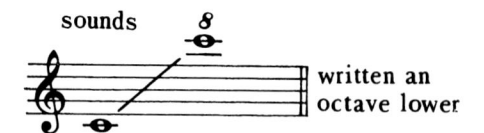

Illustrated use of both celeste and glockenspiel. (Example 86)

Example 86　　　　　　　　　　　　　　　*Variations for brass band* (R. Vaughan Williams)

9 BELLS or CHIMES
These are mallet-struck and are of the tubular type.

10 BLOCK
There are all manner of little blocks which may be introduced to point a rhythm. They have a hollow or sharp sound.

PART 2

TEXTURE

Chapter 11 TEXTURE

TEXTURE comes from the Latin 'to weave'. We have a familiar example in textile terms:
(a) the thread-material (wool, silk, glass fibre) has its individual 'feel';
(b) the threads: coarse, thick or fine;
(c) the cloth: close-woven or open like lace.

Texture in music extends to combination, arrangement, or inter-relation of structural ideas as well as to the degree of density in the weaving of parts.

As the choice of instruments and what the instruments are doing produces characteristic colours and effects, texture cannot truly be separated from that which is producing it. This works in two ways:
(1) The musical requirements of the moment suggest the instrumentation or propose a choice between possible alternatives.
(2) The nature or potential of pre-selected instruments influences the textural possibilities, eg a piano offers such resources as *arpeggi,* blurred superimposed chords using the sustaining pedal, delicately tinkling sounds in a high register which are capable of inspiring ideas differing from those suggested by a trio of trombones.

Aspects of texture are sometimes usefully analysed by detaching the considerations, as far as possible, from the sound-producing medium. For instance, contrapuntal texture is related to the manner of handling the progress and combination of parts: whilst recognizing that a vocal fugue will not sound the same as a keyboard fugue, and that the nature of the medium requires appropriate thinking, we can examine the linear technique as abstractions.

A study of compositional resources, in order to avoid confusion by having to deal with too many elements, will frequently isolate part writing (harmony and counterpoint) procedures from problems of instrumentation. In making this observation the writer does not part company with those who prefer exercises to be in terms of a performing medium whenever possible as 'paper music' tends to divorce thinking from the realities of practical performance. A monochrome reproduction of a colour painting is perfectly adequate for the study of picture composition and tone-values. Indeed it may be all the better, for this purpose, to be free from the distracting additional factor of colour. So, although we shall not lose sight of the fact that the total musical experience includes tone colour, our score analysis may, now and again, be concerned with such features as the degree of density (thickly or thinly scored) or linear (contrapuntal) character, ie the *basic music.*

By basic music is meant *what is going* on and *how,* eg:
(a) two lines in counterpoint—combined but each retaining individual and purposeful identity;
(b) an open-work 'lattice' of figures or shortish notes;
(c) the tightly-woven voices of a fugal *stretto*;
(d) block chords;
(e) a high solo line over a deep carpet of sustained bass chords.

These are just a few examples of texture:
(a) is transparent;
(b) airy;
(c) close-woven and dense if several parts are operating;
(d) solid;
(e) spatially separated elements.

In terms such as those above, the texture of a passage, seen in score, is usually visually apparent. Even at our first reading the score should convey sufficient information about such features as plentiful spaces (rests), many or few instruments playing at any given time, bars filled with busy semiquavers (sixteenths) placed high or low, a complex *tutti,* a unison or solo line and so on.

1 DEGREE OF DENSITY

To an extent the subject of *tutti* writing has been covered. It is almost too obvious a point to be made that the full complement can be playing simultaneously the parts arranged in ways which make the scoring solid (full, rich, dense) or thin (transparent). It is worth making the reference as it opens the way to a few observations.
(a) *Solid scoring:* This results, of course, from all instruments (or nearly all) fully occupied to produce a solid effect (refer to Examples 36, 37, 39, 40, 41, 45, 81, 99c, 100b and 103a).

Although the score may look solid, a four-part hymn, for instance, with the parts laid out traditionally, would not sound 'thick'. The aural density would be more likely to arise from multi-chords, especially if the middle and lower registers contained chord notes fairly close together. Careful judgement is needed to produce richness of mass without being 'muddy'. This usually arises from low harmony notes being allocated to 2nd baritone and 2nd trombone (especially the third of the chord). The comment is made, of course, in the context of the more traditional sense of harmony; thick, dense low chords may be just what the composer is out to achieve but for what it is worth—and these are often encountered in beginners' scores—the gentle warning is uttered.

(b) *Thin scoring* (refer to Example 64). Notice that, although the whole band is playing, rests thin out the texture, resulting in a much less solid effect. Also see Examples 89, 101b, 105 and 111.

Scores which have too much fussy detail or part-congestion may look impressive but can fail to give a clear impression. The strongest effects are normally obtainable with, at most, three features of interest. Beyond this the ear gives up trying to disentangle the complexities and either there is a general impression of busy but blurred activity, or the most striking feature of the moment comes to the fore. A build-up of strands in a fugal *stretto* aims at this tightly-knit bustle of sound, using it for a climactic purpose. It is not this purposeful web that is advised against but mere clutter. Backgrounds which are not intended to be too obtrusive could be an exception where patterned groups operate a kind of lacework. Also blurred or misty impressionist concepts may be the aim, the non-significance of detailed movement being a calculated totality of sound.

2 RELIEFS

Under this head come backgrounds against which a line stands out in relief:

Example 87   *Prelude on three Welsh hymn tunes* (R. Vaughan Williams)
(F.S. 209)

The sustained trombone octaves provide a static background to the bass line.

See also Example 8, a chordal stream (muted cornets) with baritone solo.

Example 26 shows flugel solo over quiet chords. In this case the effect is probably more that of a melody plus accompaniment, the prominence of the melody being largely due to its placing above the harmonic support. The example is referred to as it illustrates the principle of a differing colour helping the theme line to stand out; in this case, apart from the bass, the contrasting colour is cornet and trombone.

Were there a wider gap between the flugel and the substructure the feature would be heightened:

Example 88

3 CONTRAPUNTAL TEXTURE

As the present study is the translation of musical resource in brass band terms, comprehensive consideration of contrapuntal techniques *per se* is not a part of the scheme. At the risk of over-simplification, one may roughly say that the interest in contrapuntal writing is more in the weaving of strands (parts) and the employment of various linear devices (augmentation, diminution, imitation, inversion, etc) than in the colours chosen or allotted to the various lines. Counterpoint is horizontal thinking, maybe influenced or even governed by harmonic or vertical considerations. In a passage where two or more parts are combined there will be some degree of three elements: linear, harmonic (if only by implication or inference) and the colour of the medium supplying the sounds. The importance will naturally be relative and, in the case of contrapuntal writing, the point is made that the paramount importance will reside in the lines. A striking orchestration of the lines is bound to make its own strong impact and the characteristic colours of the instruments chosen must mostly have a bearing on the total result: a piece of *fugato* writing for two cornets and euphonium will obviously yield a different effect from the 'voices' being re-allocated to flugel, horn and E*b* bass (tuba). Of the above, rather full comment, the significant phrase is in reference to contrapuntal interest being 'more in the weaving'.

Example 89 is a basically two-part passage, for *tutti*, over a pedal:

Example 89 *The Undaunted* (Eric Ball)

4 CANON

The foregoing is also an example of canon. Canons may, of course, be developed between two (or more) instruments appropriate to the desired range and register.

The theme of Example 89 has here become a three-part canon:

Example 90 *The Undaunted* (Eric Ball)

The voices of the canonic parts are sharpened, or have their definition heightened by being differently coloured.

A three-part canon, recently encountered, was for three trumpets; each part played 'open' could confuse the part writing; by an ingenious thought of using mutes, one trumpet remained unmuted and the other two had their sound modified by a straight and a cup mute.

There is no reason why the voices should all be similar in the approach to their scoring, ie solo or *tutti*. A two-part canon, to take a voicing at random, could be between three trombones and a horn, maybe the horn doubled at the octave by soprano—the possibilities are legion. Careful thought must be given to ensure balance; balance not necessarily being equality of importance. Whilst canonic writing is conflict rather than synchronization of the strands, compositional considerations could lead to a particular strand being more prominent than the others.

Example 91 shows an inner melody with the outer voices in canon:

Example 91 — *Prelude on three Welsh hymn tunes* (R. Vaughan Williams) (F.S. 209)

5 COUNTER-MELODY

This strictly comes under the heading of counterpoint, but as its usage has been strongly developed in the countless marches to be found in the military and brass band repertoire, it is here treated separately. On page 43 we wrote of the sustained note as a binding tone. The extension of this is the familiar counter-melody, contrasting a characterful and shapely line ('melody') with a snappy figuration such as frequently forms the first subject of a march.

The counter-melody is not necessarily a tune, nor does it have to be continuous—it may be a series of phrases or shapes, the essential function looked for being the lyrical element offering rhythmic contrast. Usually the movement of a counter-melody coincides with points of rest (not always *rests*) in the main theme.

(a) *A counter-melody which is a tune,* the cornet theme being a little more pointed in character. This march is intentionally simple and is a good illustration of the principle:

Example 92 — *Toronto* (Bramwell Coles) (G.S. 1124)

(b) *A counter-melody made of broken phrases:*

Example 93 — *Dalarö* (Edward Gregson) (G.S. 1613)

(c) The converse is the *added obbligato* to a tenor theme, perhaps a march trio:

Example 94   *Silver Star* (R. S.-A.)
                                                                                                                      (G.S. 1513)

6 OSTINATO

Ostinato is a device using a recurring phrase or pattern, the word being the Italian for 'obstinate'.

Excellent illustrations of this technique are found in Edmund Rubbra's variations on 'The Shining River'; two excerpts are given below:

Example 95   *Variations on 'The Shining River'* (Edmund Rubbra)

(a) *Theme*

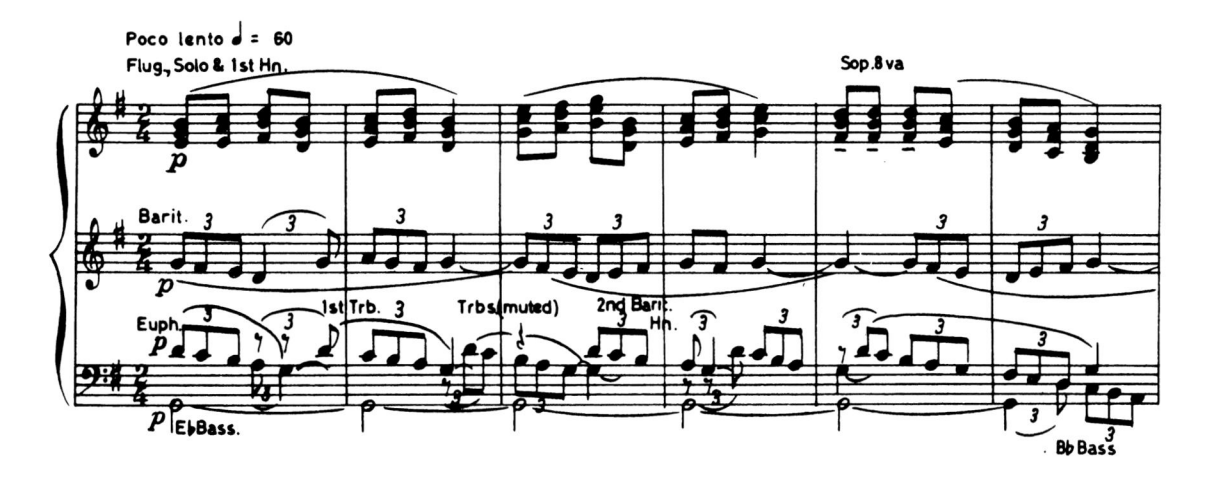

(b) *Fourth variation—Ostinato*

A further example: the patterns are maintained rhythmically for some six bars with changes of inner chord and bass part. The cornet line is constant.

Example 96 *Energy* (Robert Simpson)

A final example: bell effects using *ostinato* patterns and appropriate percussion:

Example 97   *John o' Gaunt* (Gilbert Vinter)

Chapter 12 SIX EXAMPLES OF THEMATIC TREATMENT

Example 98
A Kensington Concerto (Eric Ball)

A MAJOR feature of this work is imitative and canonic writing. The interplay of the shapely phrases and the scale figure create continuous quaver movement. Note the relationship of the cornet entry to the canonically-answering phrase (augmentation of the shape).

Example 99
The call of the righteous (Leslie Condon)
(F.S. 294)

(a)

The opening subject (a) is repeated with harmony (b). It is then 'found' to be a counterpoint to the theme played here by the trombones (c).

Example 100   *Prelude on three Welsh hymn tunes* (R. Vaughan Williams)

(a) A fragment of the minor-mode tune 'Ebenezer' in unison against slow-moving parallel triads.
(b) The same theme, following almost immediately, in a major tonality (partly whole-tone) in parallel triads; the 'line' of the chord blocks in (a) added as a decorative unison.

Example 101   *Via Dolorosa* (R. S.-A.)
                                                                                                 (F.S. 226)

A contrapuntal superstructure over a free version of 'The Passion Chorale':

(a)   a thin texture of solo parts:

(b) full ensemble:

Example 102 *The Severn Suite* (Edward Elgar)

(a) (b)

Similar basic material in two different lay-outs. Not in (a) the counterpoint to the baritone theme: soprano and euphonium two octaves apart. This an example of a double counterpoint; when encountered in (b) the subject is above flugel and baritone. The muted low G for 2nd horn is rare.

Example 103   *Prelude on 'Randolph'* (R. S.-A.)
(a)   (b)   (F.S. 246)

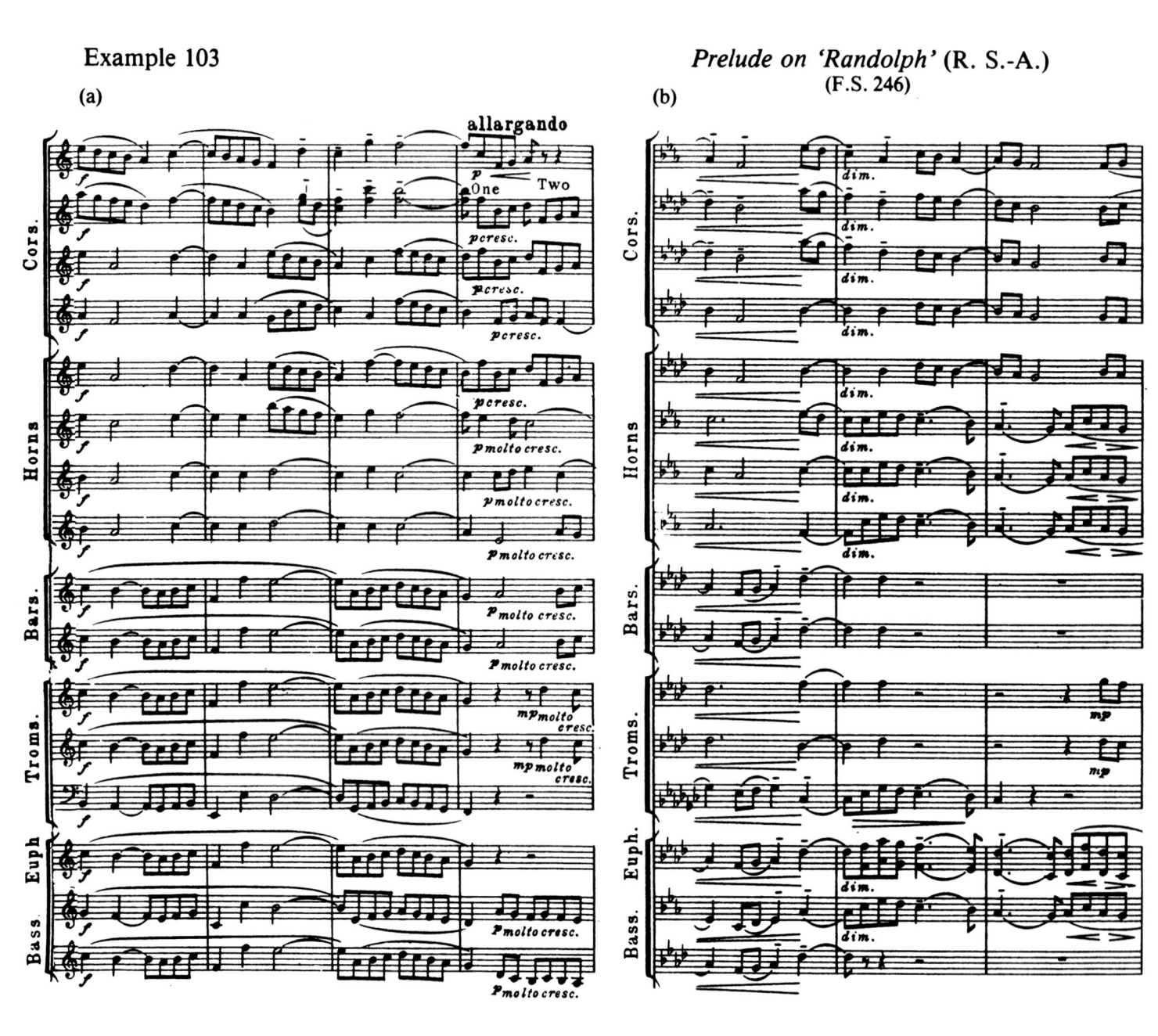

(a) A sweeping, sonorous subject in the bass under harmony and an upper counterpoint.
(b) A few bars later: the imitations are related to the upper line and general style (a). This is basically three-part harmony, the lower part of which, doubled at the octave is quite intense.

Chapter 13 FUGAL TEXTURES

A NUMBER of excerpts from fugal textures are given to show the instrumentation. They are presented without comment.

Example 104 *The Severn Suite* (Edward Elgar)

Example 105 *Variations for brass band* (R. Vaughan Williams)

Example 106 — *Gems from Gounod* (arr A. H. Jakeway) (F.S. 131)

Example 107 — *I know a Fount* (Thomas Rive) (F.S. 238)

Chapter 14 VARIOUS TEXTURES

1 'JAZZ' OR 'ROCK' SCORING

THE instrumentation of the 'big band' of the 1930s through to the present day has been brass, saxophone line, piano, rhythm including guitar (banjo) and drums. The bass line has variously been sousaphone, string bass and bass guitar. Revivals of styles or certain desired colours involve a modification of the basic group—clarinet, flute, flugel horn and so on being incorporated as required.

On the whole, the approach of most brass band arrangers, in transcribing from these sources, has been to regard the horns, baritones and euphonium as roughly the equivalent of the saxophones, the cornets and trombones being an obvious and straightforward transfer. This is only approximate because there are drawbacks. In the first place, the provision of a rhythm element by guitar and piano in pitched chords is not available to the brass band. The patterns are often allocated to lower cornets and whatever may be unemployed at the time, a fairly good solution. The back bench cornets fulfilling these and other tasks leave the solo cornet line to act as the trumpet group. The standard three trombones can be inadequate especially in close-harmony styles and this problem has to be solved. The basses, four of them and in brass, can easily make the original bass line hard and inflexible, and it is worth noting that the occasional recording has appeared which incorporates the bass guitar.

The ideal would be for a fully constituted rhythm section but very convincing scores are achieved with standard brass band resources. It is the writer's feeling that the euphonium is the most difficult to absorb. Played with its true, full, masculine tone, it seems to proclaim 'brass band' whenever its distinctive character is heard. In lower and middle register its blend is satisfactory.

Some rock singers have used brass bands of late, usually in a brass choir fashion, playing sustained chords. This is easy to transfer, less easy than any delicate piano figuration which is often included.

Basically the problem of such transcriptions is *sound*. The arranger must come to terms with the fact that a brass band playing such music will not disguise its character, and it is *sound* even more than content which is the distinguishing mark of what the general public thinks of as popular music. (These comments are bound to date, but the present book is not intended as prophecy but a review of current situations.)

Example 108 *On Parade* (Eiliv Herikstad)
(F.S. 369)

This passage occurs in the course of an imaginative arrangement of an old American folk-hymn. The instrumentation of the group providing the 'backing' to the tune illustrates further resource:

Example 109

The good old way (Bruce Broughton)
(F.S. 345)

2 TUNES WITH STRONG RHYTHMIC BACKING

Of recent years 'theme tunes' for radio, television and films are frequently strong, lyrical (folky or 'western') tunes supported by a rhythmically patterned backing, usually figures which are jazz-derived and percussive, a kind of sophisticated punctuation. The device is effective and to be found with some American brass band writers. An example by an Englishman, Edward Gregson, is taken from his variations on the Sir Hubert Parry hymn tune 'Laudate Dominum':

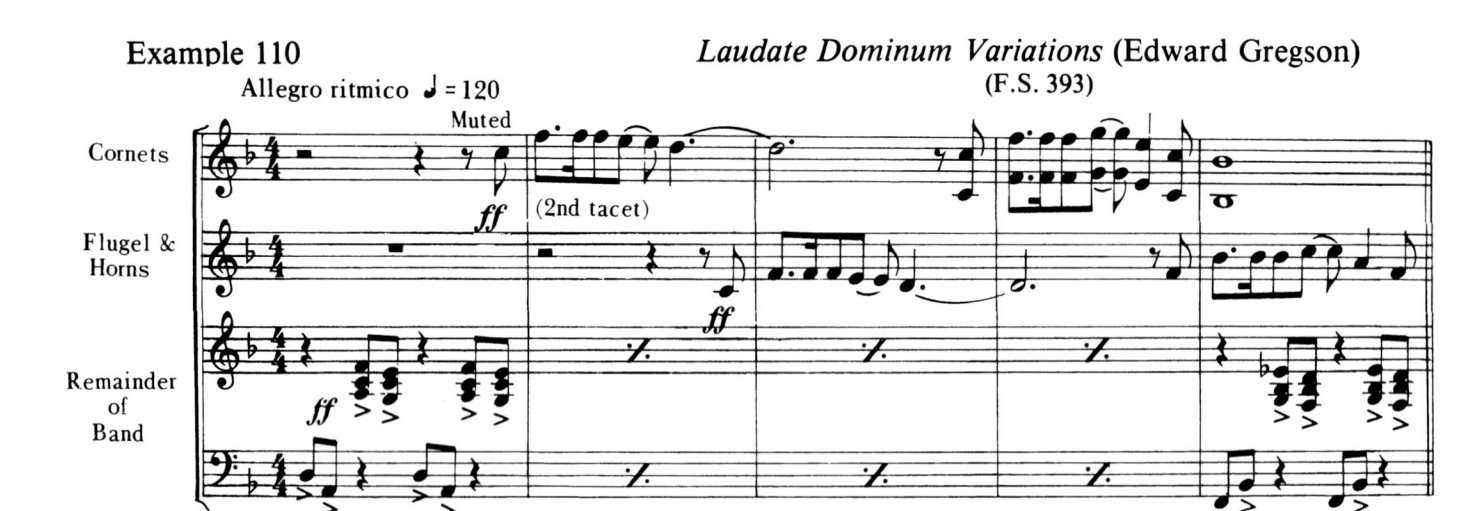

Example 110 — *Laudate Dominum Variations* (Edward Gregson) (F.S. 393)

3 COMPLEX STRUCTURES

Quite complicated-looking passages often resolve into two or three basic ideas:

Example 111 — *Scena Sinfonica* (Henry Geehl)

Example 111 is suggestive of an operatic *scene*—there are three principals; cornet, trombone and euphonium, each with an important statement.

Two streams in contrary motion:

Example 112 *Concertino for band and trombone* (Erik Leidzén)

(F.S. 211)

Abrupt changes of style and colour create tension or a sense of expectation:

Example 113

Via Dolorosa (R. S.-A.)
(F.S. 226)

4 COLOUR VARIANTS WITHIN A SINGLE CHORD

This example is, in the composer's own words, 'use of contrasting dynamics, use of changing colour and nothing else; no counterpoint, no harmonic shifts'.

Example 114   *Sunset Rhapsody* (Eric Ball)

Chapter 15 IDIOM

1 DIATONIC WRITING

THE comparative limitation of brass band colour is a discipline which has resulted in ingenious solutions. The adaptation, in brass terms, of music designed for homogeneous groups (strings, voices, organ) can often be effective—range permitting—especially where there is a contrapuntal element. A good deal of baroque, renaissance and even earlier music is currently being 'discovered' and there is quite a busy industry undertaking transcriptions into anything from quartets to full band, sometimes with brilliant results. That a work is old, or already written for a brass group of a bygone age, is not, purely for these reasons, sufficient: revivals of old music are obviously enriching, and the comparative novelty of the ancient, especially if commercially profitable (or as an antidote to what some view as brass band Victoriana) can lead to the promotion of material as artistically dubios as that of the second- and third-rate material of later periods.

The nobility of sound of a tuneful, sensitive and well-blended band will give a spacious and dignified power to even a simple hymn tune. It is a practical consideration that—at least at present—the majority of those associated with brass band music listen to and play the most easily that which is basically tonal in nature.

2 CHROMATICISM AND DISSONANCE

Music which is diatonic will usually have excursions into at least related keys, hence there will be a degree of chromatic writing, if nowhere else, then in the modulating passages. As far as writing for brass bands goes, the extra sonorities of chromatic, altered-note chords, and added-note chords, create intonation difficulties among amateur players. This means that dissonance to any degree is a hazardous path in the terms of performance. Much chromatic writing requires subtlety, particularly in impressionist directions. Of recent decades the harmonic vocabulary in band work has been greatly expanded, at times explosively so.

Dissonant chords or clusters should be carefully considered in lay-out. At this level of creative art rules-of-thumb are hardly adequate, for instance where certain chord notes are intended to have prominence.

The orchestral dictum on balance between horn, trombone or trumpet is that one trumpet/trombone equals two horns. As trombone and/or cornets increase in volume so they will increasingly tend to swamp horn sound. Multi-note chords add a new dimension of balance considerations.

As bands are rapidly coming to terms with dissonance, one finds that 'wrong notes' are queried less and less. Unfortunately this also means that misprints or mistakes sometimes can be played without question! The composer or arranger using idioms beyond the plainly diatonic has therefore to be even more careful in matters of accuracy.

3 DISSONANCE PRODUCED BY SUPERIMPOSITION

A dissonant chord can be created from the superimposition of two consonant chords played by different groups (see Example 115). The variants are endless.

Part-writing is a natural way in which dissonance arises. One encounters scores where the parts are obviously derived straight from keyboard thinking where the fingers have found the most convenient chord notes.

In the course of a long period of advising developing composers I have often needed to stress the importance of character in a part line. This would not apply in a series of block chords as it would in music of a continuous nature. If the music demands a jagged line of leaping chords, then the parts will move by leaps as the tension, colour or lay-out demands. Other than this, a shapely purposeful part is satisfying to play.

Example 115　　　　　　　　　　　　　　　　　　　　　　*Pastorale* (Christopher Mowat)
(F.S. 332)

EPILOGUE

THE purpose of this book has been to outline the proven general methods and approaches in brass band writing as currently encountered. At the time of writing a good deal of experimental work is going on, quite often being in the forms of compositions by composers not hitherto closely involved with brass bands. Hence some writing is intensely individual. *Ragtimes and Habeneras* (Hans Werner Henze), for instance, features the soprano and cornet in a principal melodic role.

New sounds and devices are bound to enrich the language and stretch players. At the same time these prophetic utterances are often 'new' more in the manner of the original music than in technical handling; the original concepts leading to combinations which seem more unfamiliar than they really are. Any composer sufficiently advanced in his mastery of contemporary techniques should be able to transfer the notation of his intentions coherently. Reference has already been made to current experiments but these do expand rather than outmode standard scoring techniques.

As with the orchestra, the history of instrumentation shows change—both by the instruments used, their development and treatment—so, even after a little more than 100 years, it is possible to see newer approaches to brass band scoring. The difference is that the basic instrumentation of the brass band has largely remained unchanged and, except in terms of the contemporary concepts which may require radical differences of handling, the majority of brass band music as received at the present day is largely faithful to the principles outlined in this book.

ACKNOWLEDGEMENTS

THANKS are due to the following publishers for permission to reproduce copyright material.

Messrs Boosey and Hawkes:
- *Energy* (Robert Simpson)
- *A Kensington Concerto* (Eric Ball)
- *Suite in Bb* (Purcell—Geehl)
- *Variations for brass band* (R. Vaughan Williams)

Messrs Novello & Co (W. Paxton):
- *Variations on 'The Shining River'* (Edmund Rubbra, arr Frank Wright)

Messrs R. Smith & Co:
- *Entertainments* (Gilbert Vinter)
- *Joan of Arc* (Denis Wright)
- *John o' Gaunt* (Gilbert Vinter)
- *A Moorside Suite* (Gustav Holst)
- *On the Cornish Coast* (Henry Geehl)
- *Prometheus Unbound* (Granville Bantock)
- *Resurgam* (Eric Ball)
- *Rhapsody in Brass* (Dean Goffin)
- *The Severn Suite* (Edward Elgar)
- *Sunset Rhapsody* (Eric Ball)
- *The Undaunted* (Eric Ball)

The remaining examples are from the publications of Salvationist Publishing and Supplies, Limited.

SA references are given as an aid in locating the full works of examples quoted.

INDEX

Acciaccatura 46
Accompaniments 36
Acknowledgements 82
Ad lib (random) 49
Arpeggio 44, 51, 54, 56
Arranging 5, 61
Articulation 46
Augmentation 39, 58

Balance 21, 24, 32, 37
Baritone 6, 8, 10-11, 14-15, 17-29, 32, 37-38, 41, 57, 69, 74
Bass 8, 11, 14-15, 70
Bass B♭ 8-9, 14, 19, 22-24, 26-29, 31-32, 34, 36, 41, 74
Bass E♭ 6, 8-10, 11, 14-15, 17-24, 26-29, 31-34, 41, 43-44, 58, 62, 74
Bass drum 51, 53
Bell effect 48, 54, 63
Bells 55
Binding tones 43, 60
Blend 32
Block 41, 51, 54, 55
Brass choir 74

Canon 4, 6, 58-59, 64
Castanets 51
Celeste 54
Change of style and colour 79
  creates tension or
  expectation 78
Chimes 51, 54, 55
Chord voicing, full band 20, 66
Chordal blocks 44-46, 48, 56
Chromatic writing 52, 80
Climax, illustration of 22-23, 39
Clusters 5, 80
Colour contrast 8, 16-17, 56
Colour variant in single chord 79
Complex structures 76-78
Contrapuntal texture 56-60, 67, 80
Cornet 8-13, 18-21, 23-24, 26-32, 37, 40-41, 44, 48, 50, 54, 57, 62, 64, 74, 77, 80
Cornet, repiano 11, 21, 23, 25, 50
Counterpoint 65, 69
  double 70, 79
Counter-melody 38, 43, 44, 60
Cymbals 51, 53

Density, degree of 5, 56
Diatonic writing 80
Diminution 58
Dissonance 80
  by simultaneous streams 77
  by superimposition 80
Doubling 14, 17-21, 37
Drum, bass *see* Bass drum
Drum, snare *see* Snare drum
Drum kit 51, 53
Dynamics 5, 20

Ensemble, full 68
Euphonium 8-11, 14-15, 17-22, 24, 26-32, 36-39, 41, 69, 74, 77

Fifths, low 20
Figure, reinforced 40
Flugel horn 5, 8, 11, 14, 19, 23-25, 27-28, 32, 34, 41, 57-58, 69
Flutter-tongue 48

Forte-piano 8, 45-46
Fugal texture 5, 16, 56-58, 71-73

Glissando 8, 44, 46, 52
Glockenspiel 54
Gong 53
Group scoring 22, 27

Harmonics 44, 47
Harmony 70
Horn 5-6, 8-10, 14-19, 21, 23-25, 27-28, 32, 34, 41, 47, 59, 69, 74, 77
Hymn tune 20, 23-25, 80

Idiom chromatic 80
  diatonic 80
Imitative figurations 35, 39, 58, 64, 70
Intensity 9, 20-21, 34, 37, 70
Inversion 58

Jazz scoring 46-47, 50-51, 74-75

Lip arpeggio 47
Lip trill 47

March counter-melody 43
Marimba 51
Martellato 48
Melody in octaves 11, 18, 19
Melody, inner 37-40
Melody line 33, 37
Melody, unison 10, 17, 37
Melody with rhythmic backing 75-76
Mutes 5, 10, 50, 52, 57, 59

Organ 23, 25
Ostinato 61-63
Overlapping 42

Parallel triads 66
Pedal, sustained 5, 9
Percussion 5, 28-29, 51-55, 63
Pitch, relative 8-9
Pitch, written 8
Pizzicato, simulated 5, 44
Pointed chords 45
Pyramid 48

Quartet 15, 19, 23, 80

Range-limit 5, 41
Reinforced phrase or figure 40
Relaxation 9
Reliefs 57
'Rip' 47
Rock scoring 74-75

Saxhorns 8, 14, 16, 19, 22, 25
Scoring, choral 26-27, 56-57
  group 27
  jazz or rock 74-75
  'male voice' 15
  solid 56
  thin 57
'Shot' note 45
Simultaneous streams 77, 80
Small band 28-29
Snare drum 51, 53, 55
Solos 35-37

Solos, backgrounds to 36-37
Soprano cornet   8-9, 20-21, 23, 29, 34, 41, 59, 69, 80
Staccato   44
Superimposition   80

Tambourine   51, 53
Tenor horn *see* Horn
Tension   59, 73, 78
Texture   5, 8, 30, 38, 44, 56, 67
Thematic treatment   64-70
Timpani   22, 51-53
Tonal contrast   16-17
Transposition   23
Tremolo   9, 44, 47-48, 53
  enharmonic   48
Triangle   51, 53

Trombone   5, 8-13, 15, 17-29, 31, 36-44, 46-48, 50, 56-57, 59, 69, 74, 77, 80
  bass   8, 12-13, 17, 19, 21, 24-27, 29, 34
Trumpet family   8, 11-14, 19, 22, 59
Tuba *see* Bass E♭ and B♭
  quartet   15
Tune with rhythmic backing   75-76
Tutti   20-23, 25-30, 58-59

Unison combinations   10-11, 17-19, 24, 37, 66

Vibraphone   51, 54
Vocal lines   23

Whole-tones   66

Xylophone   54